The No-Bullshit
Guide to Depression

Steven Skoczen

The No-Bullshit
Guide to Depression

 Ink and Feet
Paris

First Published 2016

10 9 8 7 6 5 4 3 2 1

© Steven Skoczen 2016

Steven Skoczen has asserted his
right under the Copyright Act of 1976
to be identified as the author of this work.

First published in the United States in 2016 by Ink and Feet
Ink and Feet, LLC. 1603 N. Capitol Ave. Ste 310A244, Cheyenne WY

Papers used by Ink and Feet are natural, recyclable
products made from recycled fibers and woods grown
only in sustainable forests.

Cover proudly typeset in Avenir, the masterwork of font maker
Adrian Frutiger, who lost two daughters to mental health disease,
and spent his life working to better mental health care.

Body text in Adobe Caslon Pro, by Carol Twombly.

ISBN 0-9982804-0-2
ISBN-13 978-0-9982804-0-0

for Tomo

Who got me through the hardest times
before I knew any of the stuff in this book.

With sincere apologies to all the excellent aunts
who happen to be named Dee.

Acknowledgements

This book simply wouldn't exist without the brilliant insights, talents, and support of my editor, Mary Kibbe. She brought structure to the chaos, knew when to push me and when to back off, and guided this project from a pile of raw and passionate embers into a cohesive and full-hearted whole.

You'd also find this book unreadable without the sharp eyes, patience, and humor of my copyediting magician, Devin DiBernardo. Any excessive commas, mis-used dashes and sentence fragments that remain were done over and against her explicit advice. She made every page of this book friendlier, clearer, and all-around better.

The book also wouldn't be the same without the artistic creativity and skill of Aurélie Zapatrax, whose illustrations I'm thrilled to have grace these pages. She brought life, a face, and a brilliant sense of humor to this book, and I'm joyful to have her work be a part of it.

You can thank Dr. Joe Rhinewine for making sure it's sharp, and accurate to the most recent science and evidence we have on what really helps in treating depression. His careful eyes and years of clinical experience made every page better, and like all the mental health pros I've known, he's a really nice guy, to boot.

The book (and I) wouldn't exist without my close friends and support people, who have been there for me throughout the years with depression and the creation of this book. Jeff. Seriina. Mary. Charlotte. Bonnie. The 531 gang. The guys. Amrita. Katie and Megan, who inspire me to get up every day and keep making the world better. Belle and Anya, the two most fantastic young ladies I know.

But mostly, it wouldn't exist without you.

This book is for the millions of folks who read and shared "How to Help Someone with Depression". To everyone who found a piece of themselves or someone they loved in that article, this book's for you.

Contents

People

The Long Game

WHAT'S INSIDE

Welcome

Hey there. I'm Steven. Welcome to *The No-Bullshit Guide to Depression*.

In the pages ahead, you'll get:

- the nitty-gritty someone-really-should-have-told-us-this-stuff details on depression,

- a ton of tools that really help,

- ways to handle the helpful (and super unhelpful) people in your life, and

- the confidence to know that while depression might be a part of your life sometimes, it won't define you or what you do with your life.

I wrote this book because there's a staggering gap for people like us who deal with depression.

On average, it takes us *ten years* from the time we first experience a serious depressive episode to an interaction with professional help.

For me, stubborn as I am, it was close to twenty.

In the years between, we have no real resources — just a couple of good blog posts, people around us with good intentions and usually really unhelpful actions, and blind luck.

We have to fumble our way through dealing with depression in a world that doesn't understand it, even as we figure out what exactly depression means ourselves.

And that is some serious bullshit.

This book is here to help. It's like a good lamp that won't go out, a waterproof map, and a compass. You'll still go on your own journey of understanding, navigating, and dealing with your depression — but you'll know what the landscape looks like, where you're going, and you'll have all the tools you need to take it on.

So come on in out of the rain, take this blanket, bundle up, dry off, and let's take a look around.

Inside This Book

The book has five big sections:

The Landscape of Depression We'll talk about what depression is, what it looks like in the arc of our lives, what good and bad days with depression look like, and the weird stuff that often comes with it.

Think of this section as the manual we all should have been handed when we got dealt the cards for depression.

The Pledge This is a short section, where we just commit to taking care of our depression the same as if it were any other health condition like deadly allergies or diabetes.

Tools The biggest section of the book, and packed full. In it, you'll find 60 short chapters with specific tools you can try out to take on your depression. What works is a personal thing, and everyone's depression is a bit different — so there's a huge variety in here for you to choose from, and find what works best for you.

People One of the toughest things in dealing with depression is handling the people around you who don't get it (and that's pretty much everyone.)

In this section, we'll talk through how to handle everyone from your partner and family to your boss and random strangers. We'll also walk through how to get a few awesome support people and why they are *fantastically* helpful.

The Long Game We finish up by talking about the bigger arc of your life, what depression can mean in it, building a life around the things you value, and taking on the stigma of depression in the broader world.

But before we jump in, I've got three quick notes.

#1: Dammit, Jim, I'm a Writer, Not a Doctor

I'm a writer who's lived with depression, not a doctor. Though I've consulted with mental health professionals to make sure this book isn't steering anyone down any blind alleys, it does not constitute medical advice and should not replace it.

Think of this book as a friend you meet in a bar, giving you the low-down on their life. Think of the actual doctors as doctors. Both are good to have. The friend in the bar (and this book) aren't a replacement for actual medical professionals.

#2: Dealing with Depression Right Now?

Ugh. That *sucks*. Depression is such bullshit to have to deal with.

Here's how to get the most out of this book while you're dealing with depression.

A lot of the stuff in here is about taking on your depression in the long term, and reducing its impact in the years ahead of you.

Skip all that stuff for now. Right now, it's time for some triage, getting you some energy back, and kicking Aunt Dee out of town.

Here's what I'd read, if I was picking this book up while I had depression:

1. Read the next section: "The Landscape of Depression." It'll give you the big picture.

2. Read Meet Aunt Dee (p 89), The Weird Energy-Sucking Flu (p 87) and Righteous Indignance (p 105). They're three of my favorite tools for getting perspective and getting some energy.

3. Flip through "Your Actions" (p 125), and pick out a couple that feel good. Try 'em out over the next couple of days.

4. If you've had any of the Crazy Thoughts — you know, the "I wish I were dead" kind (remember, you're not

alone in this, I've had them too) read through The Deep Dark Places (p 239).

5. If you have a person handy who you trust and who's capable of noticing and changing their actions, consider sharing the Support Guide (p 279) with them.

That's it. Focus on taking care of yourself, and getting more energy. It's never fun, and it's never easy when Aunt Dee stops by.

But she'll take off eventually.

When she does, and you're back in a good place, double back and read the rest of the book. There's a ton of good stuff to help keep her away.

Oh, and order yourself a pizza. Really, right now. It helps. :)

#3: First Time Dealing with Depression?

For most of this book, I'll be talking as if you know that depression is a recurring part of your life.

For a lot of folks, they're only picking up this book because they've been dealing with depression for years, and are looking for new things to help against the monster that's been eating their life.

But what if that's not you, and this is your first time dealing with it?

Actually, that's awesome. See, for a lot of people depression only shows up once — maybe you'll be one of them!

And "All the things someone should have told you about depression?" We're actually telling you!

Some full disclosure though: There's a chance that you'll have to deal with depression again, sometime down the road.

If you've had one depressive episode, you're much more likely to have another, so as you're reading, pay special attention to the parts on warning signs, and how to notice when it shows up.

With any luck, even if you do have to deal with depression in the future, you'll be able to skip a lot of the terrible bits, and just have your depression glance off when it stops by.

Either way, the tools in here will do you right for right now.

Let's dive in, and take a look at the landscape of depression.

THE
LANDSCAPE
OF
DEPRESSION

WTF IS DEPRESSION?

WTF is Depression?

Basically, if you've got depression, your brain is being weird.

It can be a chemical imbalance, a collection of thought patterns that have built over your life, or a reaction to external things like food, drink, or light.

Why do I have it?

Bad luck. It's usually a mix of your genes and the life you've happened to live. Basically, you got the cards for it. It's never a result of actions you took or choices you made.

Is it just me?

Nope. One in five people deals with depression in their lifetime, and one in twenty deal with it on the regular (including me). Odds are really good that you know someone else who deals with it too.

When will it show up?

Kind of when it wants.

Certain situations like loss, grief, heartbreak, and even seasonal changes can bring it on. But there aren't any guarantees, and it's different for every person.

Think of depression like a really annoying, overbearing Aunt: Aunt Dee. She rolls into town when she decides to. Sometimes, like the holidays, you can predict it. Sometimes she just shows up on a random Tuesday.

Is it the same as being sad?

Nope.

One of the biggest misconceptions is that depression is the same as feeling sad or blue (and it's one of the most annoying things we hear from the people around us — "Oh, you're sad? I've been sad before too! Cheer up!").

Depression isn't the same as sadness.

In fact, for most of us, when we're experiencing depression, we don't feel sadness as much as completely drained, numb, and like the color has been sucked out of the world.

Loads of research and brain scans back this up — depression is a completely different set of processes happening in your brain than experiencing sadness, loss, or grief — the same way that having a sneezing fit is different than bronchitis.

It's a fundamental thing happening in your brain and body, and no amount of kitten pictures will clear it out.

What's it like?

Depression is like a weird, energy-sucking flu that sometimes gives you Crazy Thoughts.

It's complete bullshit.

There are a wide range of days you may encounter when dealing with your depression.

You won't always go through all of these stages, but here's the full spectrum, so you know what you might have to deal with.

TYPICAL DAYS OF DEPRE SSION

The Good Days with Depression

Mostly, well, it's like having a weird, energy-sucking flu. On good days when Aunt Dee is in town, expect to have half the energy you'd normally have for life.

You'll feel down and sad for no apparent reason, and be more inclined to spend time on the couch reading or watching TV than out doing your normal stuff.

You'll also be more sensitive to the news, the people around you, and all negative stimulus. Those things will more easily and quickly bring you down than they normally would.

TYPICAL DAYS OF DEPRESSION

The Bad Days with Depression

A lot like the good days, but more extreme, and with some weird.

Your energy level will be maybe 10% of normal. So, if you're usually productive for ten hours a day, expect to have one good hour in you.

The sadness and down feeling will be more of a baseline state, and a certain numbness can come with it too.

Largely because of the energy level stuff, expect to spend lots of time in bed, and on the couch. It's normal to have things like eating and sleeping get weird, too.

Also, many times, the Crazy Thoughts come by. The Crazy Thoughts are things like, "Oh, I know, we should jump in front of that train."

These thoughts are like the strange thoughts that come with a high fever — they're your brain shorting out a bit, and making weird connections that result in really dark, terrible thoughts.

This entire experience is really fucked up, and the first time you experience it, you have no reference points to know that those Crazy Thoughts *aren't you.*

Here's the truth, in inarguable print:

Those Crazy Thoughts are a symptom of the weird, energy-sucking flu, and not you.

They tend to come with the territory on bad days and really bad days.

They're also one of the things we people with depression find most irritating. We're low on energy, hyper-sensitive to the bad things in the world, and on top of all that, we have to deal with crazy fucking thoughts.

It is some serious bullshit.

TYPICAL DAYS OF DEPRESSION

The Really Bad Days

These really suck. They're the most scary and they can be dangerous.

The really bad days are stuffed full of the Crazy Thoughts, often surrounded by numbness, and immense, heart-wrecking sadness when the numbness cracks.

They're awful.

These are the days where your support team can do a lot of good by giving you a space to get the Crazy Thoughts out.

Getting them out keeps you grounded that they are in fact Crazy Thoughts because of the brain short-circuits and the weird, energy sucking flu, and not, in fact, *you* or *true*.

When we're in one of these days, our judgement and decision-making abilities are really, really muddled. We're no longer reliable narrators of what's true about ourselves, our lives, or the world. Our brains are going haywire, and just like running a high fever with hallucinations, we aren't able to judge which thoughts are accurate descriptions of reality, and which aren't.

If that sounds scary as fuck, it is.

And before I get to some good news, there's one more kind of day that's even scarier.

THE LANDSCAPE OF DEPRESSION

The Weird "False Well" Days

These are the real motherfuckers.

These are days, usually after you've had some really bad days, when you start feeling better. But in a strange and dangerous way.

Your energy level will pick up, and the overwhelming sadness will be much reduced, *but the Crazy Thoughts will still be there.*

And worse — they won't seem like Crazy Thoughts. They'll seem like perfectly normal thoughts. You'll feel clear-headed, calm, rational, even.

When you have thoughts that seem clear, lucid, and grounded about jumping in front of trains — well, that's when shit gets really, really fucked up.

These days, surprisingly, are often the deadly ones.

They're also the ones that friends, family, and even support people don't see coming. After all, we seem like we're doing better.

They're days, unless we're prepared, we don't see coming either.

But there's good news. You now know they exist. When we get to finding and talking to your support people, they'll get to know they exist, too.

You can and will have support to make sure you make it

through these days too.

There's more good news. There are a *ton* of tools out there to help, and lots of good support.

Ok. Now you've got the overview on what depression is and what some of the days when it's around can be like.

It's time we talk about three big, important truths.

THREE BIG TRUTHS

Truth #1: You're Normal

This is the biggest shock to most of us after finding out that we have depression — that we're not alone.

And we're *staggeringly* not alone.

20% of people will experience a major depressive episode in their life. 5% of us will deal with depression on a regular basis.

It's more common than blond hair, freckles, or being left-handed.

You deal with depression sometimes? All good.

You get Crazy Thoughts like, "Oh, I should jump in front of that train."?

Me too. Fucking annoying, right?

Your world gets desaturated sometimes, and you just want to curl up on the couch?

Yup, me too. Lots and lots and lots of us do.

Welcome, my friend, to our giant, globe-spanning club. And help yourself to some pizza. :)

Truth #2: Depression May Never Totally Be Out of Your Life

For some people, it's a one-and-done event that takes over their life for a while, eventually goes away, and never comes back. Statistically, that type of depression is actually the most common.

But if you have that type, odds are pretty good you're not reading this book.

For the rest of us, myself included, depression comes back over and over.

It's a thing that happens from time to time, with no particular trigger, warning, or reason. Then it leaves just as causelessly as it came.

If you're one of those people, and that sounds familiar, I'm going to break some shitty news to you.

There's no "cure." Your depression is not ever likely to go away forever.

I know. It sucks. It's also complete shit that you and I and folks like us have to deal with this.

But we do. And luckily, there's a spot of good news, and it's Truth #3.

THE LANDSCAPE OF DEPRESSION

Truth #3: This Means We Can Choose to Count on It, Plan on It, and Deal with It

Just like if tomorrow you lost all your hair, you'd have two choices:

1. Deny it, and try to do the terrible comb-over thing that doesn't look good on anyone, or
2. Have a period of grief and mourning, accept it, and then make the most of your bald life.

That second choice is the good one. People who accept and own up to their baldness aren't limited by it — for some it's even a defining strength (Patrick Stewart, Sinéad O'Connor).

Baldness is simply an aspect of their life that makes some things harder, and other things easier.

This is how your relationship with depression can be.

By using the things you'll learn in this book, depression will have less of an impact on your life, you'll spend less time in the deep dark places, and you'll live more fully and more fulfilled.

But it will always be there.

So right now, wherever you are, we're going to do the biggest thing in this whole book in taking on your depression.

Ready?

Take a deep breath.

Inhale, and notice your surroundings.
Then, as you exhale,

Accept that depression is just a part of your life.

An awesome life. An authentic life. A life that happens to include depression.

Great work.

But where exactly do we start, in thinking about building this great life that happens to include depression? great life that happens to include depression?

It turns out, with our energy level.

IT'S ABOUT ENERGY LEVEL

Mostly, It's About Energy

I've got a pretty counterintuitive key for you — the most important thing to focus on when we're experiencing depression isn't making the Crazy Thoughts go away, getting ourselves out of the house, or seeing a therapist.

It's paying attention to our energy level.

Having no energy is the most crippling part of depression because it takes away our ability to get out and do the things we love. It's the component that allows depression to snowball, and the part that gets most often glossed over in discussions of the disease.

Yes, depression makes sad thoughts more present, sometimes makes Crazy Thoughts show up, and yes, it can be really scary.

But mostly, it means we're fucking exhausted.

A lot of the tools you'll see later aren't about directly affecting your mood or frame of mind — they're about freeing up more energy.

The reason is that once you've got some energy to spare, doing things to help out your mood or frame of mind become possible. Passed out on the couch, it's tough to do anything.

As you think about, observe, and learn how your depression works, pay extra close attention to your energy level, and notice things you can stop doing to free up some energy.

It's ok for us to lose a few battles. We're trying to win the war.

Spoon Theory

While we're talking about energy, I want to take a quick side road with you, and share the brilliant Christine Miserandino's metaphor for explaining and understanding the lack of energy that comes along with depression (as well as Lupus, and other affective diseases.) It's called The Spoon Theory, and we'll reference this metaphor throughout this book.

I'll outline it below, but her article is fantastic and worth a read and a share:

http://www.butyoudontlooksick.com/articles/written-by-christine/the-spoon-theory/

Imagine that every morning, you start the day with fifty spoons. To take an action — taking a shower, getting dressed, making breakfast, replying to emails, or meeting up with a friend — you have to give up a spoon.

This is what life is like for all of us, and at the end of most days, we've spent most of our spoons and we're tired.

Ok. So that's our baseline.

But what happens when we're experiencing depression is that we just start the day with fewer spoons.

A lot fewer. Like five.

With only five spoons to spend, there's no way we can get done all the things we normally do — we'd be out of spoons before breakfast!

This is why depression can so often leave us sitting on the couch or curled up in bed — we're just out of spoons, and there's nothing we can do until we wake up tomorrow and get a new set.

When we think about our energy this way, we're also able to be smart about where we spend our spoons and our energy.

We'll go into this in a lot more detail later on, but in a really broad stroke, one of the best things we can do to manage our depression is to **only spend our spoons on things that get us more spoons.**

That won't always be possible — things like work and school are insistent, and rarely give us more spoons in return — but it's a great frame for deciding what to do with the limited energy that comes with depression.

It's also a great way to explain depression to the people around us.

Alright. Now we've got the basics of what depression is and how it can play out in our lives. We also know to focus on getting more energy.

What else should someone have told you about depression? That a couple of things get weird.

THINGS
GET
WEIRD

Food Gets Weird

It's different for everyone, but odds are pretty good you're not going to be eating normally.

Some of us sit on the couch and eat tubs of ice cream.

Others of us don't feel like eating at all.

A few of us even do both. :)

Wherever you fall on the spectrum, it's totally ok, and you're completely fine.

Let yourself do what comes naturally, and unless it's really strongly impacting your health, don't spend energy fighting it.

This is *depression is in town*. It's not *forever*.

Sleep Gets Weird

Yep. Sleep gets weird too.

Just like food, it can go either way. Some of us sleep for hours and hours and hours.

Other folks lie awake all night.

And some lucky few do both.

You might find yourself in either or both extremes as you move through a visit from depression — and that's totally fine.

Just like the weirdness with food, your best bet is to just accept whatever weirdness is happening with your sleep schedule, let it work itself out, and save your energy for something else.

As depression leaves town, your sleep schedule will generally swing back toward normal on its own.

Your Sex Drive Gets Weird

Yep. It's super, super unlikely that your sex drive is staying normal.

For a lot of folks, they're not in the mood for between-the-sheet romps of any kind.

This is really intuitive for people experiencing depression, and super unintuitive for their partners.

They're all, "But I was sexy yesterday! What gives?"

And you're all, "The world is drained of color and I'm reasonably sure I'm now part sea slug. Sea slugs are asexual."

They do not understand this.

For other folks, depression can increase their sex drive. And a few people — you guessed it — get both. Their sex drive both increases and decreases, in cycles.

If any of these happen to you, don't worry.

These changes are completely normal, and they happen to all of us.

Once depression leaves town, things will swing back.

Everyday Stuff Is Exhausting

As we talked about a few pages ago, a huge component of depression is the lack of energy. But the way that plays out is weird.

I've had afternoons where I thought I was feeling better, got up, took the trash out, and found myself *exhausted*.

I took two bags of garbage outside and came back inside.

I've run triathlons, I eat right, and my body is not yet falling to pieces. Taking two bags of garbage outside should not exhaust me.

But it did.

This happens, and it's totally normal. You may find that things that were no big deal now take some planning. Happens to all of us. Things are weird.

Relationships Get Weird

One counterintuitive thing about depression is that our relationships and interactions with other people change, in unexpected ways.

There are people who we love deeply and are close to us who are *terrible* to be around when we're depressed. And there are friends we're not actually that close to who happen to be fantastic supports.

The reason for this odd effect is that we're often told that *closeness* and *helpfulness* are the same thing. But they're not.

Take a look. Here's a pretty typical spectrum of *closeness*:

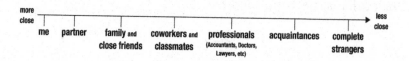

However, the *helpfulness* of these people changes, depending on the situation. For instance, if you really had a tough tax question, your helpfulness spectrum might be like:

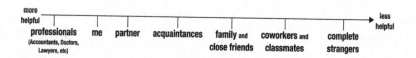

And there would be a point, probably just past your partner, where talking to people about your tax question would actually be *unhelpful*.

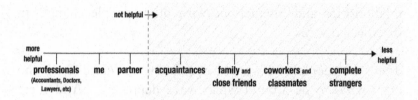

All of those people past the dashed line would still be happy to give their opinions, and they'd be really well-intentioned, *but they wouldn't be helping*.

This same dynamic is true when depression's in town, and the order will change depending on the kind of day you're having.

Let's say you're having a "good day" with depression. Your helpfulness spectrum might be:

But on a bad, or really bad day, it might instead be:

Knowing that the helpfulness of the people around you changes when depression is in town can make it easier to decide where to spend your time and energy (remember, only spend your spoons on things that get you more spoons).

We'll talk about this a lot more in the people section of the book. But for now, just know that when depression is in town, your relationships are likely to shift around a bit. This is totally ok, and completely normal.

That's the Landscape

In this section, we've talked through the landscape of depression.

What it is, how it might show up, and the ways it can play out in our lives.

We've taken a look at the sorts of days you might experience with depression, and what they're like.

We've talked through three big truths:

1. You're normal.
2. Depression may never be gone for good.
3. You can count on it, plan on it, and build an awesome life that includes occasional visits from depression.

We talked about the most important thing to focus on when dealing with depression — energy level — and you picked up the awesome Spoon Theory metaphor.

Finally, we walked through how depression can make food, sleep, sex, relationships, and everyday stuff a kind of weird.

This is all the stuff someone should have told you when you got the cards for depression. Finally, someone has.

Next up, let's take a minute and talk about the most critical step in taking on your depression, and the mind-frame you'll need to take it on.

THE PLEDGE

THE PLEDGE

You're In Charge and You're Responsible. Both.

Depression can be hugely disempowering. There's weird shit happening in our brains, giving us Crazy Thoughts and stealing our energy.

But here's a big truth: Your depression is not *you*. It's a thing you're dealing with, like the flu or a sprained ankle. It sucks while it's there, but with care, it will eventually get better. I promise.

There's an awesome thing about that truth — it means that you're still in charge. You're still *you*, and you make the calls.

But just like that sprained ankle or the flu, it also means you're still responsible for taking care of yourself. Depression can be a motherfucker, and just like the flu, if untreated, it can kill you.

Your job is to not die.

Take it seriously, and you'll be just fine. As a bonus, your depression will typically take off sooner.

But what do I mean by, "seriously"? I mean make a commitment.

Commit to Take On Your Depression.

You're reading this book, so you've given it a start. That's awesome.

But to really get to that awesome life where depression is just an annoying thing that happens from time to time that you've got the tools to handle, and to avoid and survive the deep, dark, scary places, you need to go further than that.

You need to treat your depression like it's diabetes or deadly allergies.

You need to dig in, put in effort to find and hone tools that work for you, have important conversations, and build support systems around you.

You need to commit to take your depression seriously.

To put real time and effort into it, consistently.

To make it one of the core things you do in maintaining your health.

You *can* have an amazing life filled with the things you love, in which depression plays no more of a part than passing storms.

But it won't happen on its own, and it won't happen without some effort.

This is the *No-Bullshit* Guide to Depression, remember. I'm not here to fluff you up with platitudes.

But if you're ready to seriously take on your depression, and reduce its impact on your life, you can *absolutely* do it, and this book can help.

If you're ready to change depression's impact on your life, right now, out loud, I want you to say the following sentence:

"I am committed to take on my depression. I am willing to do some difficult things, show up consistently, and work to master my tools to deal with it."

Awesome. You've just done a big thing.

In the long-term, the commitment you just made is the biggest thing you'll do in changing depression's impact on your life.

Now let's get some tools in your hands to help you take it on.

AWESOME TOOLS TO DEAL WITH DEPRESSION

Building Your Toolbox

Living with depression is like living in a beautiful old house with poor plumbing. There's a gorgeous breakfast nook overlooking a garden, bright wide living room windows, and high ceilings with lovely exposed beams. It's a wonderful house.

But the pipes are a bit wonky. Living there, you know that every once in a while, a pipe is going to burst, there will be water everywhere, and you'll need to fix it and deal with the damage.

Living in that house, you'd quickly invest in proper tools for doing plumbing work. You'd learn to identify leaks early, when to patch, when to replace, and what to do when a pipe bursts in the wall during a sudden rainstorm.

You'd have a go-to toolbox, a nice one with strong sides and good handles, full of all the things to handle your plumbing problems. You'd have the sizes that fit your hands, and worked with your house's particular problems. Wrenches and clamps. Spare sections of copper and PVC. Teflon tape and sink traps. You'd be ready for it all.

You'd probably even start doing some preventative maintenance as time and money allowed, and become friends with a local plumber to up your skills, to make life easier for yourself down the road.

Sure, the plumbing problems would inconvenience you, but they wouldn't ruin your life, or your breakfasts overlooking the garden. They'd just be plumbing problems that happen sometimes, and you'd have the tools to handle them.

This book will help you build a toolbox just like that, but focused on dealing with your depression.

We'll talk through a variety of useful tools, and you'll try them out and pick out the ones that really work for you. By the end, you'll have the tools to notice, respond, recover, and to build an amazing life that happens to include your depression.

Let's begin right now, by physically building your toolbox.

This will be the place you write down *the things that work for you* and keep them handy for when you need it.

It can be a physical notebook, a document on your computer, or a note on the wall. All that matters is that it fills these three criteria:

1. You can add to it at any time.

2. You always know where it is and you can get to it when you need it.

3. It's something you can make *yours*, with your own personal style.

Right now, before we move on, go ahead and start your toolbox.

Title it. Name it "Gwen's Bad-Ass Depression-Fighting Toolbox" or whatever fits your fancy. Give it some personality. Make it *you*.

Finally, find a home for it where you'll always know where it is.

Great work. Now, let's find some tools you love and fill it up.

Types of Tools

Broadly, I've broken out the tools into similar groups:

- Using Your Mind
- Things You Can Do
- Using Your Body
- Changing Your Environment
- Tools to Notice Depression
- Tools for the Deep Dark Places

For each tool, you'll see what it's good for, why it works, and how you can put it in practice.

Try them out in your life, see what works for you, and find the ones you really love.

Ideally, you'll end up with a few tools from each section — a mix of all the types to fill up your well-rounded toolbox.

Let's jump in!

USING YOUR MIND

Introduction

In this section, we'll look at tools that live inside your mind.

These are things that nobody else knows or can see, that change how you interact with your mind and the world.

They're like secret ninja weapons. You can pull them out in a meeting or a classroom. On the bus. In line at the checkout. In the middle of a conversation. Of all the tools in this book, these are some of my favorite and most-used.

Let's start off with the two best metaphors for depression I know — the Weird, Energy-Sucking Flu, and Aunt Dee.

The Weird, Energy-Sucking Flu

What it is:

A frame for seeing your depression, and explaining it to other people. You've got the weird, energy-sucking flu. You'll be better eventually, but right now, it sucks.

(A *frame* is a psychological technique that provides a structure to organize your thoughts and experiences — a kind of scaffolding in your mind. They turn out to be pretty helpful in taking on depression, and we'll introduce a few of them in the pages ahead!)

What it's good for:

Two things.

First, it's great for giving yourself perspective — reminding you that depression is something that's happening *to* you, instead of *being* you.

Experiencing depression is just like getting bronchitis or a terrible, hard-to-explain rash in your groin. It's a really annoying thing that's happening to you — but it's not who you are.

Second, this frame is really useful for explaining depression to other people. People who don't deal with depression, often think it means you're "blue", that you have sad thoughts. Since they have sad thoughts too, they think they get it. But they don't.

By using "energy-sucking flu" to explain and frame your depression, they're able to start to understand that depression isn't actually mostly about being sad. It's about having no energy, some sadness, some weird thoughts, and all the repercussions of dealing with all that shit in a world that can't see, identify, or understand what you're dealing with.

Why it works:

Metaphors are hugely powerful things. Inside our brains, they physically change the way we relate to and understand the world, and ourselves.

By giving yourself (and the people around you) a really solid, easy-to-understand metaphor for depression, you're able to treat your depression for what it is — a super-annoying, energy sucking-flu.

How to use it:

For yourself:

When you notice you're experiencing depression, treat yourself just like you would if you got a bad flu. Take care of yourself, know it will probably pass on its own, and give yourself a break.

For other people:

When you talk about your depression, bring this metaphor in, early in the conversation. It will let people latch onto an accurate and clear description, and shift out of super unhelpful patterns.

Meet Aunt Dee

What it is:

Another frame for seeing your depression, and explaining it to other people — Aunt Dee has come to town.

Imagine your depression as a giant, ugly, domineering aunt who has just burst into your home and is setting up in your room.

Her voice sounds like scratches on chalkboards. She's stinky, unshowered, and wearing a bright floral print dress that is neither stylish nor suitable. Her dental hygiene leaves a lot to be desired. And she has moles. Lots and lots of moles.

She's self-centered, demanding, controlling, and super annoying.

She is the face of your depression.

It's completely unfair that she's stopped by and ridiculously annoying.

But there are rules.

She can't actually touch you or control your actions. She can talk and wail and be super irritating on the couch, but she can't physically control you or what you do.

You can't make her go away, but she can't do more than jabber and be really annoying to you.

And you can say whatever you want to her, without fear of repercussions.

Meet Aunt Dee.

Whenever you're dealing with depression, imagine her as the self-contained embodiment of depression, and then do whatever you want to do in that reality.

What it's good for:

Giving your depression a face you can look at, talk to, and get pissed at.

Aunt Dee is different than the energy-sucking flu because it's a personally relatable frame, and you can talk to it. Talking to the flu is a little surreal. Telling Aunt Dee to get her stinky ass the hell off your couch is completely reasonable. I mean, seriously. We just cleaned that couch.

Why it works:

Just like the energy-sucking flu, Aunt Dee gives us a powerful metaphor for understanding our depression that frames it accurately.

It gives you (and the people around you) a way to see depression as an annoying thing that's happening to you (and mostly out of your control), instead of just some sad feelings that will go away with enough kitten pictures.

How to use it:

Make a description of Aunt Dee in your toolbox. Write. Draw. Collage. Get creative. Make her ridiculous. Make her make you laugh. And make her real.

Get detailed about that floral print dress. Note what foods she always pilfers from your fridge. Jot down her favorite annoying phrases. Get a full, broad picture of what she's like when she stops by.

Then, when your depression comes to town, pop open your toolbox, remind yourself what Aunt Dee's like, and speak your mind.

Tell her to stay out of the cheetos, and that all her blabbering about you not being any good is just her being bitter that her floral dress is ugly and *so* 1971.

When sad or dark thoughts come by, imagine she's the one saying them. You can even try it out loud, saying thoughts that show up in her voice.

Give your depression a face you can look at, talk to, and become exasperated with.

That's the key — it's depression. It's not *you*.

Radical Acceptance

What it is:

A concept from psychology where you accept — *radically, man* — everything about how you find yourself and the world around you for what it is, in this very moment.

What it's good for:

Those times when you're stuck in an endless thought loop, or having really strong emotions.

Why it works:

Feedback loops of emotions and thoughts happen to all of us, and they can get bad, quick.

Radical acceptance short-circuits the entire process.

Let's say your thoughts are like, "Oh, I'm a failure for not doing more," and your emotions are raging, "Sadness! Guilt!" The feelings prompt more couch-sitting, which prompts more failure thoughts which gives more sadness and guilt — we all know how this goes.

Radical acceptance says, "Hang on. Ok. Right now, I'm experiencing thoughts that say I'm a failure for not doing more. I'm currently feeling strong emotions of sadness and quite a bit of guilt. I'm currently sitting on the couch, in my living room, and I can hear the heater and some traffic from the street. I can see my living room, and it's half-dark because I haven't turned on the lights. Anything else? Nope. I think that's it. That's what's happening."

And I bet right now, as you read that, you get why it works.

It's a powerful dose of cold-water reality that re-grounds you, and puts agency back in your hands.

How to use it:

1. Start by taking inventory of everything you're experiencing, and the world around you. Here's some questions to help you cover the bases:

   - What kind of thoughts are stopping by? How long are they staying?

   - What emotions am I feeling? Get specific, and identify each one.

   - How does my body feel? Go through each body part. How are your feet? Your knees? Your back? Your earlobes? Take inventory of your physical experience.

   - What are my sensory experiences? Go through each sense, and make mental note of everything you can notice. What are all the sounds you hear? What are all the smells you experience?

2. With all of those experiences, with all that's with you in the present moment, take a deep breath in.

3. Then, as you breathe out, accept that those experiences are just where things are right now. The future will be its own thing, and the past is done, but right now, this is where you find yourself. Ok.

4. Present, grounded and accepting where you are in this moment, ask yourself, "What would I like to do next?"

Rephrase It

What it is:

A super-cool, easy psychological trick that lets you change your relationship to what you're feeling, just by describing it differently.

Instead of saying, "I'm sad", just say, "I'm experiencing sadness."

What it's good for:

Rephrasing is a great habit to get into whenever depression's in town. With one simple tweak to how you phrase things, you give yourself space from your experience and open up the possibility that what you're currently feeling will pass.

Why it works:

Rephrasing works because of how the brain appears to construct identity.

When we say things like, "I am sad", we're reinforcing (quite literally, in our brains) the idea that *who we are* is a person who is sad.

When we instead say, "I'm experiencing sadness", we construct an identity independent from sadness, where sadness may come and go, but *we* still remain.

That little difference plays out in some really big ways because of how our brains appear to construct the concept of who we are. Instead of the static, never-changing *me* we feel like we have, research is showing that we're a lot closer to a big ball of stories.

And if we can tweak the stories, even with little things like the above, we actually tweak who we are. Pretty crazy, huh?

How to use it:

1. In your bad-ass depression-fighting toolbox, make a page for "Rephrase It."

2. Think of the three most common emotions you feel when depression's in town.

3. Write out all three, with the original and their rephrases, like the examples below.

   ~~I'm sad.~~
   I'm feeling sadness.

   ~~I'm hopeless.~~
   I'm feeling hopelessness.

   ~~I'm exhausted.~~
   I'm feeling really low on energy.

4. When depression rolls in town, re-read those three. Then, when you notice yourself using "I am _____" phrasings, just mentally rephrase it to "I'm feeling/experiencing ____". That easy.

Let Yourself Off The Hook

What it is:

A conscious way to acknowledge and then put down the "I shoulds" and guilt that often come along with having less energy.

What it's good for:

It's completely logical and reasonable that while depression is in town and we're low on energy, we're going to get less done.

But often, it doesn't *feel* reasonable. A lot of us deal with guilt, anxiety, and the weight of an increasing to-do list as the days go on.

Letting yourself off the hook allows you to put those emotional burdens and extra tasks down.

In turn, it frees up energy you can use to help yourself out.

Why it works:

The list of to-dos often comes with a sneaky side-effect: guilt for not having gotten things done.

When we're dealing with depression, this combination can snowball, sapping our energy and our mood.

But by letting ourselves off the hook, we stop the cycle and get a clean break.

How to use it:

1. Make a list of all the to-dos that are piling up. Do a full brain dump, and get all the things that are running through your head down on paper.

2. Think through any errands or sundry tasks (laundry, cooking, and email replies) that you could either hand off or stop doing for a week or two. Add them to your list.

3. When you're done, read through the entire list.

4. Then take a deep breath — and let it go. It's not getting done for a little while, and that's ok.

Just like if you were stuck in bed with the flu, it's ok to put down all the busy tasks of life for a little while.

All the important stuff will still be there when depression has left town.

Mindfulness

What it is:

A millennia-old practice for hacking your brain.

You've certainly heard of mindfulness — it's everywhere these days. But what the hell is it?

Basically, it's a way to practice focusing your awareness on what's actually happening right in front of you, and getting some space from your thoughts.

Sounds pretty useful for the crazy, soul-sucking thoughts that show up with depression, right? It is.

Even better, it's backed up by everything from millennia of human experience, to modern research papers and MRIs. It works.

But there's a catch.

Contrary to popular explanation, mindfulness isn't actually about the experience in a particular moment. It isn't a tool to magically make you feel better *right now*.

Instead, it's about changing the structure of your brain, slowly, in the long game.

Having a mindfulness practice is like going to the gym. You don't go to the gym to be strong and look good *in the gym*. That would be crazy. You go to the gym to be strong and look good in *the rest of your life*.

Mindfulness works the same way. Building a regular mindfulness practice — even a few minutes a day — will slowly change how you think, and give you more and more ability to pause, get out of your thoughts, and notice the world around you.

For me, in the long-game, it is *the most effective tool* in my toolbox.

Every morning I wake up, start the coffee, do my mindfulness practice, then get coffee. Every morning. On good days. On bad days. On days I feel like shit. On days I'm raring to go and ready to take on the day.

That consistent practice, over years, is what's changed my brain. If you put it into consistent practice, it will change yours too.

What it's good for:

Like good vegetables, mindfulness can help you out in more than one way. Things like:

- Making depression more manageable and less intense in the long run.

- Making it easier to get perspective and experience strong emotions without them overwhelming you.

- Making it easier to be present in the moment, and get out of your thoughts.

Why it works:

Mindfulness physically changes the structure of your brain. Here's some of the research-backed changes that have been observed:

- A more developed *anterior cingulate cortex* — this is a part of your brain that's associated with your ability to willfully focus your attention and behavior, and suppress knee-jerk responses. *Yep, that's helpful in dealing with depression.*

- Increased function and grey matter in the *hippocampus* — a part of your brain involved with emotion and memory. (Notable: folks who deal with depression and PTSD often have smaller hippocampuses, and that's thought to be a part of what causes both conditions.) *Yep, helpful in dealing with depression.*

- Reduced grey matter in the *amygdala* — a part of your brain connected to anxiety and stress. *Yep, less stress and anxiety is helpful in dealing with depression.*

- A wide variety of behavioral changes, including in perception, body awareness, pain tolerance, emotion regulation, introspection, complex thinking, and sense of self. Studies also show links to decreased blood pressure, increased attention span, and increased empathy. *All pretty solid.*

How to use it:

1. Start a daily mindfulness practice right now, and then again first thing tomorrow morning — just 2 to 5 minutes will do it.

2. Find a time that works for you each day. I recommend first thing in the morning (I do mine while the coffee is brewing), since nothing can have come up yet, and you'll have the time each day.

3. As for the specific structure, there are a ton of apps, YouTube videos, books, and websites to provide guidance.

   Try a few, pick the one that works for you, and stick with it. The important thing is the practice itself, not the program you use.

4. Here are my favorite resources for mindfulness:

   iOS Apps:
   Mindfulness Daily (This is what I use)

   Android Apps:
   Calm
   Headspace

   YouTube:
   3-Minute Mindfulness:
   inkandfeet.com/3-min

   Read:
   Jon Kabat-Zinn's guided meditation scripts:
   inkandfeet.com/zinn

   Carol Vivyan's mindful breathing scripts:
   inkandfeet.com/vivyan

Then, once you've found a method you like, day after day, just keep it up. :)

Righteous Indignance

What it is:

I love this one. Righteous Indignance is simple. In the face of your depression, just allow yourself to get really fucking pissed that it even exists.

What the fuck kind of bullshit disease takes your energy and gives you Crazy Thoughts? This is complete and utter bullshit!

Righteous Indignance can work even in the darker, deeper trenches of depression, by connecting us to the reality that our brain *is going fucking crazy* and *that that is such bullshit*.

I've used it to pull myself out of some holes, in a surprisingly powerful way.

So dig in, allow yourself to get pissed, rant, and hold up a big middle finger to depression. You might find yourself with more energy on the other side.

What it's good for:

Giving yourself a boost of energy and some perspective on depression.

Like Aunt Dee, Righteous Indignance focuses our vitriol on depression itself, not us.

Why it works:

Getting angry (actually angry) will fire off a set of hormones in your brain — things like adrenaline and testosterone increase and cortisol decreases. Our heart rate rises, and our senses are heightened.

From an energy-management standpoint, all those changes translate into a little extra boost of energy and motivation.

When that boost is coupled with a good perspective (I am me, and depression is around right now, and seriously, fuck that shit), we can find ourselves up, doing things that we care about, and engaged — and those actions can help knock down the effects of depression.

How to use it:

1. Take a deep breath, look your depression in the eye, and then let it rip.

2. If you want, write out a full-throated rant. Here's a bit to get you started.

Dear Depression,

Fuck you.

Fuck you for _____

and

Fuck you for _____

and

Especially super-fantastic fuck you for _____

I didn't ask for you, want you or need you in my life. But you know what? I'm going to make a great life despite you.

Take that.

Important Note: Make sure to keep that anger and energy focused at your *depression*, not yourself. If you're in a place where you don't feel a strong separation between yourself and your depression, save this tool for another day. It'll still be there when you need it.

Get Grateful

I know. In a book that promises not to be filled with fluffy platitudes, I have a chapter on gratitude? When dealing with depression? I know. But it's backed up by so much research, and is so easy to do, I had to put it in the book.

What it is:

Taking a few moments to focus and list things you're grateful for.

What it's good for:

Getting perspective, and more importantly, rewiring your brain.

Why it works:

The perspective-getting is pretty straightforward. We're confronted with things we really like that are around us, and reminded that, despite the Crazy Thoughts and the general greyness of reality, those things exist.

But the more interesting part is what's happening inside our brains. Our brains work a lot like our muscles — the pathways we use more often get stronger, and it's easier for us to use them. The ones that we use less take more effort.

You've seen this in effect when you recall a random name or number you use often, but struggle to recall a childhood address or phone number. The pathways in our brains that we use get developed and maintained. The ones we don't fall into disrepair and get harder to access.

Making a gratitude list tells our brains that the pathways to things that make us feel grateful and fulfilled are important, and that our brains should build those pathways and make them stronger.

It's a technique that can help us both in the moment we use it, and over the long term. A win-win for us and our brains!

How to use it:

1. Make a list of five things you're grateful for. It's that simple.

2. If you do this on an ongoing basis, try adding in some constraints, to make yourself stretch and build new mental pathways. Here are a few:
   - Two of my five things must be ones I haven't named before
   - Five things outside my house I'm grateful for
   - Five things from (faraway place) I'm grateful for

3. Keep it going. To make the effect bigger, repeat this on a regular basis. Get into a habit every morning. In the middle of a visit from depression, consider doing it a few times throughout the day.

Tip: Sometimes, on the harder days of depression, you might not *feel* grateful (or much of anything for that matter).

In those times, you can still use this tool, but instead of looking through a gratitude lens, make a list of things you care about, or things and people you'd protect from destruction if you had the power.

You'll get the same brain-reinforcing effects, even if you don't have all the feels.

Let Go of the Rope

What it is:

A frame for looking at depression that lets you stop fighting it, and start living your life even though it's around.

This one's a bit like Radical Acceptance, but specific to your depression. It comes from a scenario I was shown by a therapist.

Picture yourself on one side of a deep, deep chasm. This chasm is the Deep Dark Place, the scary, frightening, dangerous part of depression.

On the other side of the chasm is a giant scary monster. It is depression. It's strong, scary, and genuinely dangerous.

Between you and the monster is a rope. You're both holding it tight, and it's trying with all its might to pull you in.

You're fighting back, spending all the energy you have to keep from toppling over the edge. It's working, but exhausting.

Then someone walks by, and points out another way.

"Hey. Why don't you let go of the rope?"

Hunh.

You let it go, and it falls harmlessly to the ground.

The monster is still there. Big, and scary and shouting for you to pick up the rope.

The abyss is still there, frightening, dangerous, deep.

You're still right next to it.

But instead of spending your energy fighting the monster, you can spend it doing something else. Like working in your garden. Or creating art, or working on things that line up with your values.

You'll still be low on energy, and you'll still have sad thoughts.

Your depression will still be there, yelling, insisting that it's going to pull you in, and egging you on to grab the rope and fight back. But you don't have to.

You don't have to pick up the rope.

What it's good for:

Getting perspective that while depression might be in your life, big and scary and sucking all the color and energy out, you don't have to spend your energy fighting it.

They're your spoons. Spend them however you'd like. Try as it might, depression can't make you pick up the rope and fight it.

This tool is also useful to use more than once, as we'll often "pick up the rope" without knowing it. When you notice that depression feels giant and overwhelming, it might be time to think about dropping the rope.

Why it works:

This frame is effective because it short-circuits the stories we have around depression, and reminds us of our big, broad life, in which depression (loud and scary as it may be) is just one part.

How to use it:

Note: If you can find a person to physically do this with, it's a wonderful experience. If not, you can get the same benefits from doing it in your mind.

Here's the steps:

1. Have a partner stand across from you, and each of you hold one side of a rope, cord, or whatever you can find.

2. Mentally imagine that there's a deep abyss between you. It's the deep dark place, and you don't want to fall in.

3. Now, your partner's job is to pull on the rope, trying to drag you in.

4. As they pull, notice that your instinct is to pull back, and do it. Pull hard. This is completely normal, and natural to all of us.

5. But after a bit, as they're pulling, just drop the rope.

Feel that?

You can do that with your depression, too. Accept that it's there and trying to be scary. Then stop fighting, and instead spend your energy doing things that you love, and things that give you more energy.

Present Moment Awareness

What it is:

Simple as it sounds. Notice what's happening in the present moment, right in front of you.

What it's good for:

Getting out of your head!

I use this one often — and not just for depression. It works on anxiety, runaway thoughts, even those brain-dead zombie times when I've forgotten to eat.

Why it works:

By putting our focus into our physical senses, we reconnect our minds with what they're telling us about the world around us, and our actual place in it.

Some of the toughest places in depression come from vicious circles of thoughts in our heads — we have dark or hard thoughts, which makes us feel worse, which gives us even worse thoughts, and the cycle goes on.

Research has shown that the emotional impact (our hormonal and chemical responses) to our *thoughts* are just as strong as *external reality*. To our brains and bodies, thinking about being chased by a cheetah is as bad as *actually* being chased by one. We're not weak or messed up because we're impacted by our thoughts — it's just a function of how our brains work.

But we *can* do something about it. By turning our mental focus back into our senses and the world around us, we give our minds a different narrative.

I have toes. I'm in a room. It's actually rather dark in here. Hm. I guess I should turn on a light.

How to use it:

Here are two approaches: one goes sense by sense, and the other goes super-deep on just one sense. Both are effective, try them out and see what you like best!

<u>One sense exploration:</u>

1. Pick one sense — your sight, sound, smell, feel or taste — and decide to focus in on it.

2. If you can, tune out the other senses. So, for example, if you're focusing on sound, close your eyes.

3. What is the first thing you notice? The most intense and obvious stimulus? Notice those first, loud notes.

4. Then, go subtler. What's behind those notes? What else can you hear, feel, smell, see, or taste?

5. What's the quietest thing you can hear? Or the smallest detail of something you've not looked at closely? What does the bottom of your little toe feel against it?

6. Be methodical, and explore everything you're taking in through this sense, from loudest all the way down to

smallest and quietest.

7.   When you're done, open yourself back up to your other senses. Welcome back. That's the world that's all around us, all the time. :)

Sense by sense:

1.   Stop what you're doing, and bring your attention to your hearing.
     • What sounds do you hear?
     • Which ones are loud?
     • What are the softer sounds?

2.   Now, turn your attention to your feeling of touch.
     • What do you feel?
     • What sensations are intense?
     • What are the subtler, less strong sensations?

3.   What about smell?
     • What are the strongest smells nearby?
     • What are the subtle ones, hidden in the background?
     • What other things can you smell?

4.   What about taste?
     • What do you taste?
     • What are the tastes at the tip of your tongue?
     • What about the back?

5. Finally, bring your attention to sight.
    - What are the things near to you?
    - What details do you see in them, looking closely?
    - What things do you see in the distance?
    - What do you notice about them now?

6. When you're done, open yourself back up to your other senses. Welcome back. That's the world that's all around us, all the time. :)

Stalk It

What it is:

Get in touch with your inner Sherlock Holmes, and just stalk the hell out of your depression.

When does it show up? What's it do? What does it try to convince you of? What feeds it? When does it shut up? What is it obsessed with? What does it like? What does it hate? How does it eventually leave?

Become an expert in your depression like the world has never seen. Take notes. Take them several times a day. Learn its cycles and moods, and what makes it tick.

What it's good for:

Actually, stalking your depression is great for two things:

1. It helps you really understand what *your* kind of depression looks like, how it works, and that lets you game plan and counteract it effectively.

   You'll learn what helps and what doesn't. (For example, despite loving music, I've banned myself from listening to a half-dozen albums when depression is in town. They really, really don't help.)

   You'll become familiar with how it approaches, and how it leaves, and learn more and more how to handle it.

   But that's not all.

2. Just by switching your role to observer, you're reframing in the same way we've done throughout this section.

   Just like if you kept getting the flu, you'd pay attention to what might be increasing your risk of catching it, and you'd get really good at recovery.

   Depression is something annoying that happens to you. When you stalk it, you treat it this way.

Why it works:

The reframing effects work in the same way as Aunt Dee or the Weird, Energy-Sucking Flu.

But the stalking and taking notes component also engages your analytical, problem-solving brain. That hands you agency over the things you can do, and puts you back in a place of being able to learn, plan, and eventually take action.

How to use it:

1. Take notes in that bad-ass depression fighting toolbox you started at the start of this section.

2. Every time Aunt Dee is in town, note:
   - The date
   - What it was like? Be as detailed as you can.
   - What made it better?
   - What made it worse?
   - What kinds of thoughts are around?
   - What tools did you try, and how did they work?
   - What else would future you find it useful to know?

3. When depression has passed and you're in a good place, some sunny day pull out your tool book and look for patterns. Do certain things seem to attract it? Are any tools particularly effective, in hindsight?

4. Pat yourself on the back, doff your imaginary pipe, and congratulate yourself on a job well done, Mr. Holmes.

This rounds out the tools for your mind. Now, let's get out of our minds, and take a look at some actions.

YOUR
ACTIONS

Introduction

This section is all about things we can do that can help get us more energy, provide outlets for the stuff that runs around in our heads, and keep us engaged with the stuff we love.

If you're going to spend your spoons on something, this section is a great list of places to start.

Order Pizza

What it is:

Just what it sounds like. The day you notice Aunt Dee is in town, order a pizza from your favorite place.

If you don't like pizza, order Chinese food, Thai food, or whatever kind of delicious delivery they offer in your area.

For the next few days, just order in, and take that off your list of things you need to worry about.

What it's good for:

Saving your energy for things that can help you out, and keeping your body well-fed.

Ordering in your favorite food takes one more thing off your list, and will make sure you've got things you really like, even though food might get weird.

Why it works:

Fundamentally, because pizza is delicious. It's not much more complicated than that. :)

But structurally, because it's a simple tool to ensure you have a good source of nutrition that won't cost you any energy to make, that you're actually interested in eating.

It seems basic, but the basics are what give us a great foundation to get through depression's visits.

How to use it:

1. Think of your three favorite places to order delivery.

2. Then, in your toolbox, write out their name, phone number (or website), days and hours, and your favorite dish that feels the most like comfort food.

   It might seem silly, writing out stuff you could just look up online.

   But in those rough days when you're low on energy, having done the above is three more decisions you won't have to make.

3. If money's a concern on ordering food, (and it is for all of us), tuck some cash in the back of the book to cover three orders of your favorite food.

Now, when depression rolls into town, your food needs will be all set — and that will make a huge difference.

Dial It Back

What it is:

As we've talked about throughout this book, managing your depression is mostly about managing your energy.

At the worst parts, you'll be at 10% of what you can normally do. In better times, you'll be at 50%. 80 or 90% is not happening.

That's ok. Eventually, your depression will pass, and you'll be back to your superhuman self.

But in the meantime, it's time to cancel what you can and lower what you're asking from yourself.

That stressful networking event? Ditch it.

Cancel social engagements. Opt out. Say no.

Cancel all that you can — including things like cooking meals, getting the mail, doing laundry, and anything else you can manage.

The truth is, most things in life can either be skipped entirely for a short period of time (getting the mail, doing laundry), or you can pay someone to get them done (food delivery, yardwork).

Take advantage of that truth, and offload all the big stuff you can.

Pick off small stuff, too. Turn off email notifications on your phone, and only check it once a day. Tell friends you're slammed and that you'll get back to them in a couple weeks.

Put off anything that takes willpower and energy until you're back to full strength.

What it's good for:

Conserving your spoons for the stuff that you really want to do, that gets you engaged, passionate, and interested.

Why it works:

Our big goal with dialing it back is to take that 10% or 50% energy level you have, *and put it towards things that help you.*

Your health, creativity and passions don't get the dregs left after you've finished the yardwork. By cancelling all the routine maintenance of life for a bit, we're instead able to give them the very best of your time — right off the top.

How to use it:

1. In your awesome book of tools, make a page for "Things I Can Stop Doing when Aunt Dee is in town," and then fill it up.

2. Think through last Wednesday, and make a list of everything you did. Then, cross out the stuff that you could skip if you really needed to. Start your list with that.

3. Now that you can see some examples, fill out the list with other stuff you can skip for a little while.

    Here's some suggestions to help you out:
    - Yardwork
    - Dishes
    - Laundry
    - Cooking
    - Replying to Email
    - Checking Facebook or Twitter
    - Getting the mail
    - Turning off notifications on my phone
    - Running non-essential errands
    - Cleaning
    - Going to social events

4. When depression rolls into town, pull out your list, and just cancel all the stuff on that list for a period of time. Maybe it's a week, maybe two. Give yourself a specific and defined break from all of it, and save that energy for something else.

Eat a Salad

What it is:

Ok. I know I just said to order a pizza. But hang in there.

Do order the pizza. Also, eat a salad.

And not some lame iceberg and carrots with ranch nonsense. A serious salad. Get some spinach or kale in there. Eat the biggest, leafiest, dark-greeniest salad you can get your hands on.

What it's good for:

Getting more energy, keeping our brains working well, and providing a great baseline for our body to recover and work well.

Why it works:

Brain chemistry. Our brains need lots of things to run well, and some of them are oddball minerals and vitamins that don't tend to reside in pizza.

The single best place to get all those neurobiologically necessary molecules? Dark leafy greens.

Depression is some weird wiring going on in our brains. But sometimes, just giving our brains and bodies the stuff it really thrives on can make a huge difference.

How to use it:

It may sound crazy, but give it a shot some time. Make a note of your mood, have a salad with lots of leafy greens, and then six hours later, measure your mood again.

<u>If you like salads</u>:

Find a favorite salad recipe (or restaurant that has an awesome salad) that includes dark, leafy greens.

Then, in your toolbox:
1. Write down the recipe, step by step.
2. Write down the grocery list you'd need to get to make it.
3. Tuck a bit of cash in the back of your book to cover the ingredients.

<u>If you hate salads</u>:

No worries. Go full smoothie.

1. Find a nearby smoothie stand, and order the greenest thing on the menu. Something with spinach or kale or something that was once leafy and deep, dark green.
2. Try stuff until you find something green that you like.
3. Write it down in your bad-ass depression-fighting toolbox:

   Smoothie Hut on Lombard and Kigali way. Green Monster. $4.99

4. To remove excuses, tuck some cash in the back of your book to cover two smoothies.

Next time Aunt Dee rolls into town, cover her in green. :)

Practice Kindness

What it is:

I love this tool. It seems counterintuitive, but it really works. Practice kindness.

This means intentionally being extra-kind to people, wherever you find them. On the internet. At the grocery store. At work or school or home.

What it's good for:

Being kind is another of those marvelous things like gratitude that actually has effects in our brains. When we're being kind, we report higher senses of clarity, grounding, and happiness.

If that sounds like a nice trifecta to take on depression, it is.

Why it works:

While it's obvious that all of us feel great when people treat us with kindness, what's not so obvious is that being kind ourselves does similar favors to our brains.

Research has shown that people who are intentionally practicing kindness — just being extra nice to the folks around them — report higher levels of satisfaction, happiness, and engagement with the world.

Brain scans back those self-reports up. Intentionally being

extra-kind fires up the parts of our brain associated with connection, empathy, and satisfaction — a pretty handy trifecta in taking on the grey, isolated space of depression.

How to use it:

Depending on what kind of day you're experiencing when you try this, I'd be a bit mindful of where you practice kindness.

Practicing with terrible trolls on the internet means that you'd also be exposed to a lot of negative, mean thoughts, and the overall balance probably wouldn't be good.

But practicing among friends, strangers in public, and people you know will generally go well, and give you energy and a lightened mood.

Here's how to try it out:

1. Make a list of five people or places where you could practice kindness.

2. Then, when depression rolls into town (or even before that), pick one of them, give it five minutes, and give it a shot.

3. When you engage, focus on the *feeling* of kindness, and then take actions that bring you closer to that feeling. It's slightly different than the feeling of helpfulness, politeness, or niceness. Focus in on *being kind*, and let it shape the space you're in.

Behavioral Activation

What it is:

A frame that helps you do things that you believe in, *even while* you feel bad.

A few years ago, I saw a graph that changed my life. Yeah, a graph. Seriously. Hang in there.

Here it is.

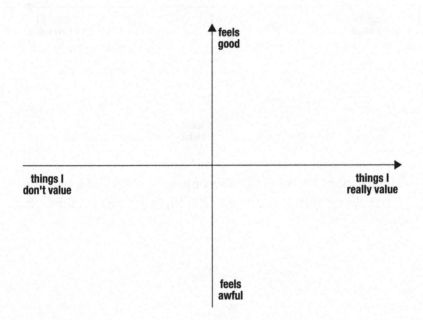

From left to right, the graph is about whether something is in line with your values, and the things you believe in.

From bottom to top, it's about how you feel.

Ok now we've got the layout. We easily can imagine things that fit in all four corners.

Say, for example,

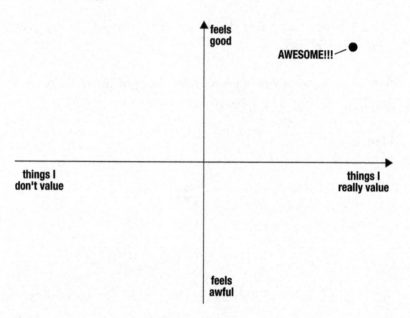

The top right corner is the awesome spot. You feel great, and you're doing stuff you care about. That's where we all love to be.

And then there's this:

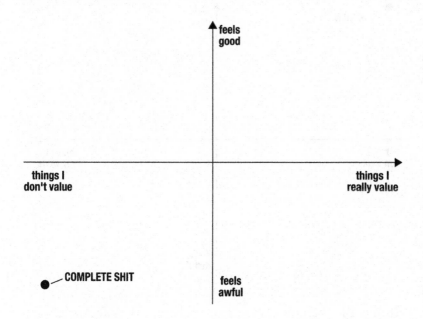

The bottom left corner is the shithole. You feel terrible, and the things you're doing go against the things you believe and value.

Then there are the weird spaces. Like the top left corner.

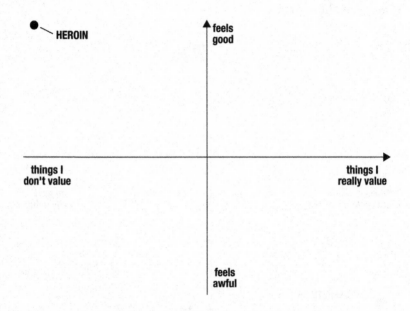

Things like heroin tend to live up here. They feel great, but pretty much nobody woke up with "being a junkie" as one of the things they valued and wanted to do with their one precious life.

And then there's the bottom right corner.

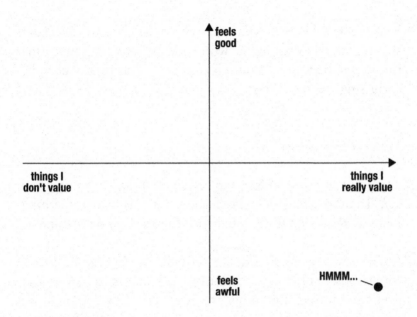

The one where we feel terrible, but we're doing things we believe in, and strongly value.

Stuff down here actually turns out to be a great way to take on depression.

It's an idea called *Behavioral Activation* in the psychology literature, and in essence, it just boils down to "do stuff you believe in, even though you feel shitty."

For me, this graph unlocked that *how I feel* and *what I do* are not necessarily linked things.

It's possible for us to have a rough day with depression, feel like shit all day, and still go out in the world and *do the things we value*.

Will we feel better? Maybe, maybe not. But we *will* have spent that day creating a world we believe in, supporting the things that are core to who we are. That turns out to be surprisingly empowering.

What it's good for:

The point of this tool is *not* to say "suck it up." It's instead to say, "In those times when I'm feeling shitty, is there something I can do that is totally aligned with the things I believe in?"

Intentionally going and doing activities we believe in does a couple powerful things. It means that one more day of our lives went toward the things we cared about, even though we deal with depression.

You may or may not feel better that particular day. But studies have shown that in the long-run, Behavioral Activation is one of the best tools to take on depression and reduce your overall symptoms.

Even better, it also upends the stories around depression.

Why it works:

Behavioral activation powerfully shakes the narratives that depression likes to tell about itself and us. Narratives like "I'm no good" or "I can't do anything" or "Everything is meaningless."

It proves, through action, that we are people who act on the things we value. It makes sure that those values and actions — not the fact that we deal with depression — are what define us.

How to use it:

It's important to note that behavioral activation won't magically get you any more spoons. Instead, it's saying that instead of spending your valuable energy doing the dishes or scrolling facebook, you'll spend it volunteering at a local shelter, or contributing to something you really care about.

For most of the things in this section, we've focused on saving your spoons up for something that matters. *Behavioral activation* is where you spend them.

Here's how to set yourself up:

1. In your book of awesome tools, make a "Actions I believe in" page.

2. On it, list five tangible things you could do in the world that *you really, truly believe in.*

   Maybe it's volunteering at a local nonprofit. Maybe it's picking up litter. Maybe it's tutoring someone, tending your garden, or spending quality time with a friend or family member.

   Think of five things that you really believe in, and make them well defined. "Spend one hour volunteering."

"Talk to Jenny for fifteen minutes." Give yourself an action that you can complete, and know when you're done.

3. When depression rolls into town, and you're ready to try behavioral activation, pick one item off that list.

4. Before you do it, take a deep breath, and accept that by the time you finish, you may not feel any better. Then commit to complete this one task anyway.

5. Get out there, and do something you believe in. Screw you, Aunt Dee. You're not the boss of us.

Talk to Yourself, Your Dog, Your Plants, or a Rubber Duckie

What it is:

Talking. Not to another person *per se*, but out loud.

Talk to yourself.
Talk to your dog, your cat, or your goldfish.
Talk to your plants.
Talk to the rubber duckie you keep in the bath.

Whatever you pick, find something to talk to, and start talking.

Talk about the things you're feeling, how they come and go, and what you're noticing about the current place you're in.

Talk through your hopes and your fears, and get the thoughts that keep running around out of your head, then talk about what you think about them, now that you've gotten them out.

What it's good for:

Talking — even to ourselves — helps us process our experiences and gain perspective on our thoughts.

If you're stuck with thoughts running in a loop, try talking them out.

Why it works:

There's research that indicates that having to vocalize and physically move our bodies to speak changes the way we think about ideas, and changes our relationship to our thoughts.

The physical process of speaking appears to directly affect the way we understand ourselves and our thoughts.

While talking to a good listener is great, we can also get those same physical speaking benefits by simply talking to yourself, a pet, some plants, or an inanimate object.

And don't worry if you feel self conscious about talking to yourself — lots of us do it, a lot of the time. It's perfectly normal. :)

How to use it:

Computer programmers often talk about "rubber duckie debugging." That is, they explain the problem they can't figure out to a rubber duckie, and in the process of doing it, quite often the problem becomes apparent.

Some even have physical yellow rubber ducks on their desks.

To give yourself the tools to make this one easy, decide what you're going to talk to, when Aunt Dee rolls into town. It can be a specific inanimate object, a pet, or a plant.

For this one though, don't make it a person. We'll get to support people later — they're awesome — but what you want with this tool is something you can just talk to, and get it out.

Pick your object, look it in the face — or leaf — and start talking.

Write or Journal

What it is:

Write. Whether you free-write on a scrap of paper or create a regular journaling practice, writing is a great way to get perspective and understanding.

What it's good for:

Just like talking, writing is great for getting distance from our thoughts, perspective on what's happening, and an outlet for all the things that often get bottled up in our heads.

If you feel like there are things filling up inside you, grab a pen and get them out!

Why it works:

Writing and journaling has been shown to be one of the most powerful tools in combatting depression, because it gets the thoughts out of our heads, and into an external place where we can see them.

Putting pen to page gives us an outlet for those thoughts, and the ability to step away from them. Literally.

Writing also has all kinds of neat neurological side effects, including the ability to detach from our emotions and see them as something that we experience, instead of a core part of our identity.

If you write consistently, you'll also create a positive habit and outlet for your thoughts, and easily be able to see changes in your depression over time.

How to use it:

Writing about all aspects of your life and your depression will give you the most clarity. The bad. The good. The Crazy Thoughts. The annoyances and the shitty and well-meaning "support" that so often comes from the people closest to us.

There's no wrong place to start writing, and no wrong topic to start on. When you sit down to write, if you've got something that comes to mind, start there.

If you draw a blank, here are a few prompts to get the ball rolling:

- I feel...
- The most annoying thing about all of this is...
- The best part about today was...
- The hardest part about today was...
- Next week...
- When I look out the window...

You can write about anything — from narratives of your life to complete fiction. It all helps.

Start a Creative Project You Love

What it is:

Start a new, creative project, in a medium you love.

Maybe it's writing, collage, scrapbooking, knitting, drawing, filmmaking, cooking, painting, music, or any of the hundreds of other art forms out there.

Whatever your particular favorite is, start a new project in it, and let yourself enjoy it.

What it's good for:

Many folks (me included) find that a creative project actually gives us *more* spoons. I've found myself, even in some bad days of depression, able to spend hours fiddling away on an idea I'd always wanted to make but never justified the time for.

If you're looking for a way to increase your energy level a bit, starting a creative project (that you love) is worth a shot.

Why it works:

The opposite of depression isn't happiness. It's passion. It's active, engaged, vital energy.

By focusing your time on a creative form that you enjoy, you're engaging the parts of your brain responsible for creativity, movement, and action. Just like the tools we covered back in *Using Your Mind*, this can have really positive impacts.

Working on a creative project also tends to wake up all kinds of habits and memories and passion that can light a fire in you and swing you up from depression into an active, creative space.

It won't make Aunt Dee vanish from the couch. But it can make you forget that she's there.

How to use it:

1. Pick your favorite medium, or one you'd enjoy trying out in the moment.

2. Get out whatever supplies you need and whatever tools will help you create.

3. Start making. You can begin with a goal in mind, or just start on a small corner and see what happens. Let yourself focus on the *creating*, and see where it takes you.

Find Your Pizzas and Enjoy Them

What it is:

Related to "Order a Pizza", but more metaphorical.

Find the actions that take no energy and give you comfort and support.

For me, eating pizza does make that list. It's delicious, gives me dinner (and breakfast!), and makes me feel happy and comforted. As a bonus, a person who requires no energy from me will deliver it for a very reasonable fee.

But there are other things on my list as well. Things like video games, watching *Star Trek*, writing, cleaning the house, and listening to music.

Your list is likely to be different. Find the things that work for you, and use the energy you have to engage with them.

What it's good for:

Finding a way to fill your time that doesn't take any spoons, leaves your mood as good as you found it or better, and gives you a sense of comfort.

One of the things that can snowball our depression is all that time exhausted on the couch, with nothing but the weird thoughts to keep us company. Find some company you like better, and keep it instead.

Why it works:

Finding ourselves with 10% of the energy we'd normally have doesn't mean that we only have 10% of the hours in the day.

Sure, we'll often sleep more when depression is in town, but not *twenty hours* more. So what happens with those other hours?

They get filled up with our rambly thoughts or whatever we stumble upon. But if we set ourselves up with things we love that also relax us and pick us up (me, I'll binge-watch *Star Trek* yet again), we can find ourselves on the other side of those hours in no worse shape than we started.

In the grand scheme of depression coming and going, that's a huge win.

How to use it:

1. In your depression-fighting toolbox, make a list of some things you love doing that take no energy, and generally leave you in a better mood than you started.

    Tip: Be aware that things like darker movies or books are likely to hit you harder when you're depressed. You don't have to make a fluffball PG-rated list, but do keep that in mind as you make your list.

2. When depression's in town, try them out, and see what works. If you remember, make a little note on how they worked, and if you found them helpful or if you found another way to spend your time.

3. *Don't* use this as an excuse to try to "be productive" or "get something done with your downtime." Let yourself off the hook. This stuff is just to recharge you, and help you wait out the storm. Let it just be that.

Alright, that covers some great action-based tools you can use. Next up, let's dive into the root of all of this: your body.

YOUR
BODY

Introduction

Fundamentally, depression isn't some weird ethereal state caused by the ghosts of Christmas past being vengeful.

It's your brain and body being a bit weird. So, a great place to take it on is right there, starting in your body.

Balance Your Diet

What it is:

We're back on food again, but for good reason. It's what our bodies, marvelous machines that they are, run on. Food is great place to invest our energy, since it will almost always give us more in return.

Balancing your diet is as simple as looking back at what you've eaten in the last few days, seeing how your balance has been, and seeing if there are any adjustments that could help.

If it takes more than a minute or two of thought, you've overthought it.

What it's good for:

As we've talked about, food gets weird.

It often goes one of two ways: either we eat a *ton* of carbs and sugars (related to our hibernation instincts, interestingly), or we don't eat enough.

By taking a quick moment to check in and see what we've been eating, we can make sure our bodies have what they need to support us.

Why it works:

The reason isn't the simple "eat your vegetables" schtick we heard from society. It's that our body and brain need nutrients to run properly, and they need them double when we're dealing with depression.

Just like if you had the flu, you'd make sure you were eating well and drinking lots of fluids. Same goes for depression.

How to use it:

In short, just make sure you're eating a healthy balance, and notice what you're putting into your body.

If you're eating a case of donuts every day, add in a salad or some Thai food.

If you're not eating as much as you normally would, order a pizza, or have some of your favorite food.

Keep it simple, kind, and relaxed. Here's a quick checklist, if you'd dig a little more structure:

1. With an eye just to notice, think through what you've eaten in the past two days.

2. Think back to what you were eating a couple of months ago, and mentally compare. Are you getting some veggies? Eating enough protein? Enough food in general?

3. If you notice that anything is missing, think of the simplest way you could add that food to your day, and jot it down.

4. If you notice things that are extra, think of the easiest thing you could swap out or add for more balanced

foraging.

5.   If you're eating more than normal, generally, don't stress about it. But *do* make sure that you're still eating some quality fruits and veggies. Your body will be fine with some extra carbs or ice cream, but your brain really needs those vitamins and minerals.

6.   Once you know what you'd like to adjust, make it happen just one day this week, and see how you feel.

     The marvelous machine that is your body will thank you — and you can thank it right back. :)

Go for a Walk

What it is:

Walking is magical. It's the single most validated activity to lengthen your life, improve your mood, up your IQ, and improve your health.

It's simple, easy, and you can do it pretty much anywhere.

Walking turns out to help depression, too. A good walk releases lots of helpful chemicals into our bloodstream, gets us in contact with a broader world, helps us get space from our thoughts, and can strip away some of the haze of depression.

Weirdly, it also doesn't take much energy past getting out the door.

What it's good for:

Just about everything.

Getting a little boost of energy, getting out of your thoughts, and getting perspective.

Going for a walk helps out on almost all of the symptoms of depression.

It's cliché, obvious, and something your grandma might have told you, but when in doubt, go for a walk. It will almost always help.

Why it works:

Our brains appear to have a deep relationship with walking (and running, for that matter).

Walking releases lots of helpful hormones in the brain that help things like memory, learning ability and mood, while decreasing anxiety and stress response.

Walking in natural environments has even more benefits, with studies showing significant decreases in activity in the part of the brain known as the *subgenual prefrontal cortex* — the part responsible for the aptly-named "morbid rumination" process — a way of brooding where we run through our thoughts over and over.

A simple walk can physically change what's happening in our brains, and for the better. If you can get yourself walking, do it.

How to use it:

In practice, it's as simple as putting on some shoes and walking out the door. But to make things a bit simpler and give yourself a little nudge, you can also make a plan:

1. In your toolbox, add a page for "Go for a Walk", and put two entries below it.

2. The first is a route for a five-minute walk you could take.

3. The second is a route for a twenty-minute walk.

4. When depression rolls in, take a look at how much energy you have, and decide if you're up for the five minute or twenty minute variety.

5. Then lace up your shoes, and just get yourself out the door. Your brain and legs will do the rest.

Work Out or Go for a Run

What it is:

Go for a run, or get a good, hard workout in at home or your local gym. Break a sweat, and get your heart and adrenaline pumping.

Almost any kind of exercise will do, from a long brisk walk to intense cardio or weightlifting.

For my money though, I prefer something intense, that pushes me into an aggressive, almost angry place.

As we talked about back in Righteous Indignance (p 105), anger can be a marvelous tool in taking on depression, by bringing us energy, and shifting the narrative around what's happening.

A good, hard workout can be a great way to get it in.

What it's good for:

A boost of energy (exercise is one of those rare things we can spend our spoons on that gets us more spoons), and an equalizing effect on our moods.

If we make it a good hard workout, we can also get the benefit of our body's get-up-and-go responses to stress.

Why it works:

Endorphins are powerful things. They're the chemicals in your bloodstream that make you feel pleasure, reduce pain, and generally feel awesome. How awesome? Chemically, they're similar to morphine, the crazy loopy painkiller.

Workouts of any kind are going to kick in your sympathetic nervous system, and give your body and brain lots of feel-good chemicals. Studies show vigorous workouts as short as six minutes are effective in taking on the symptoms of depression.

But whatever form you choose, working out is an almost sure-fire way to get your *body* to do its part in fighting off your depression.

How to use it:

1. In your bad-ass depression fighting toolbox, list out three different workouts you can do.

2. Get specific. If you're going to a gym, which gym? What will you do there? How long will it take?

3. If you're running or biking, what's your route, and how far is it?

4. Anticipate obstacles and how you'll handle them. What's your plan if it's raining?

As you're probably noticing, we do a lot of planning ahead in these *how to use it* sections.

That's because minor difficulties that would be easy to handle normally get a lot tougher when depression is in town and we're low on energy. Anticipating what could go wrong, and making a simple, step-by-step plan for ourselves to follow is a big, big help.

Laugh and Smile

What it is:

Find a way to get yourself genuinely, belly-achingly, laughing.

What it's good for:

Laughter (the belly-jostling, uncontrollable kind) triggers all kinds of lovely chemical and neurological changes. It makes us feel happier, more connected, and makes it relatively easier to have light thoughts, and harder to have dark ones.

Why it works:

Again, it's back to biology. Laughter creates a cascade of really positive effects in our bodies.

It relaxes our muscles, releasing physical tension and stress. It releases endorphins and serotonin, the body's natural mood-boosters. It fosters a sense of connection, reduces anxiety, and even helps prevent heart disease.

Cliché as it may be, laughter really is quite the medicine.

Most importantly, laughter can have long-term effects on our brain chemistry — both helping us feel better in the moment, and increasing the odds we'll wake up with more spoons and fewer negative thoughts tomorrow.

How to use it:

It doesn't matter what you're laughing at, as long as you get laughing.

Find the things that really get you giggling, and jot 'em down in your depression-fighting book. Here are some ideas to get you started:

- Sophie Scott's TED talk on "Why We Laugh"
- Youtube vine compilation videos designed to make you laugh
- Youtube videos of baby goats
- Funny books
- Stand-up comedy
- Videos (yep, really) of other people laughing
- Playing with a pet
- Reading comics
- Talking to an old friend who always makes you laugh, and recalling funny situations

Note: Your experience might be different, but for me, when depression's in town, I find things like political satire (which I usually enjoy) a bit too far on the "the world is a fucked up" side, and less on the "this is really, really funny." Your experience may differ, but keep an eye out — things you normally enjoy might strike you differently when depression's around.

Eat Spicy Food

What it is:

Eat some food that's a little spicier than you normally would. Get yourself sweating.

What it's good for:

Similar to the effects from laughter or going on a run, eating spicy food kick-starts our adrenaline and sympathetic nervous system, and gives us a little boost of energy both now, and further on down the road.

Why it works:

Spicy food has a funny effect on our bodies — it releases endorphins — the same kind of feel-good chemicals we get after a run, sex, or feeling pleasure.

The mechanism is simple. The capsaicin in the spicy food binds to heat receptors on your tongue, and to the reptilian parts of your brain, *your tongue is literally on fire.*

As a result, it fires off all kinds of chemicals to help put the fire out and cool you down — adrenaline, endorphins, and the lot. Really spicy food makes us sweat, causes our eyes to water, and elevates our heart rate.

And that combination of chemistry is actually really helpful for depression — it's a physical pick-me-up that improves our mood and sets the stage for us to have more energy tomorrow.

How to use it:

Don't worry. You don't have to drink a bottle of hot sauce or bite into a habañero pepper to kick off your brain's spice reflex and get those endorphins.

Our tolerance to spice is completely relative. If you don't eat spicy food often, a mild curry or some mustard may do the trick.

If you're a spice junkie, you'll have to step up to a higher level of Thai, Indian, or Mexican food.

Your benchmark is this: eat something that's *a little more* spicy than you usually would.

If you get a little forehead sweat and reach for that extra glass of water, that's perfect.

Lighting your taste buds on fire to fight off Aunt Dee — who knew, right?

Take a Cold Shower

What it is:

Take an ice-cold shower. I know. It sounds like zero fun. But it really can help.

What it's good for:

Taking a cold shower provides the same effects as eating spicy food or going on a run — but more dramatically.

It can improve our mood, fight off dark thoughts, and increase our energy level. A little cold, it turns out, goes a long way.

Why it works:

Finding ourselves suddenly in icy water makes our bodies react powerfully, with a variety of chemicals that all have the side effect of fighting off depression.

It raises our heart rate, dumps beta-endorphin and noradrenaline into our systems, and appears to overload the part of our brain associated with decreased mood.

It's been shown to be quite effective in reducing the symptoms of depression, without causing any dependence (big shocker there — who gets addicted to cold showers?!)

Just like everything in this section, we're triggering our own body to help us fight off depression — and it's very much up to the task.

How to use it:

1. Turn the water on super cold.
2. Get in.
3. Yell, probably a lot. :)

It really is that simple, but if — like me — the idea of jumping into an ice cold shower seems impossible, the studies we have on the effect show that it works just as well if you gradually decrease the temperature of your shower over five minutes.

You're looking for a temperature of about 20°C (68°F) for about two or three minutes.

Steven's Note: Because I love you, and because it'd been a while since I'd tried it, immediately after writing this chapter (and in the middle of a visit from Aunt Dee), I got up, walked into the shower, turned the cold water on high and got in.

Three minutes (and a lot of "eek" and "aaaaah" and "oh dear gods") later, I stepped out — shivering, but also laughing, with my mood lightened. It's ridiculous, but it really does work.

Give it a shot once, and see how it works for you!

Use Feldenkrais or Somatic Learning Methods

What it is:

Felden-what? Exactly.

Feldenkrais and somatic learning are methods of awareness similar to mindfulness.

But instead of starting with the brain, learning and awareness starts physically, with your body.

The overall effect in your life is similar — you'll find it easier to pull out of your thoughts and into the present, and have more options for how you respond to situations.

But the way in is very different. If you're an intensely physical person — someone who's always felt that your sense of touch is your strongest sense and connection to the world — Feldenkrais can be a great choice.

What it's good for:

Like mindfulness, it's a long-term tool.

It won't be something you'll necessarily pull out in the middle of a bad day of depression, though it won't hurt. Instead, somatic learning methods can give you greater awareness of your mind and body, and thus more ability to respond.

Why it works:

Deeply grounding our experience in our bodies and physical sensations pulls us out of our thoughts, and into the world around us.

But these methods can also teach us new ways of viewing the world, using our mind and bodies, gaining perspective, and finding resilience.

It's learning, just like you're doing now, but in the language your body speaks.

How to use it:

There are a huge number of somatic learning systems out there, and any number of them could work well for you.

I personally enjoy and have benefited a lot from the Feldenkrais method (funny name because it was a dude's last name), and it's reasonably wide-spread around the world.

To try it out, you can look for a class in your area, or find one online. There are "Awareness through Movement" group courses which tend to be cheap, accessible, and a great place to start. You can look for a class near you at:

http://www.feldenkrais.com

If you don't have a session near you, there are now also a few practitioners offering virtual sessions. Here's one that I recommend:

http://www.feldenkraisclasses.com

Do Sports, Yoga, or Martial Arts

What it is:

Running or going to the gym can be a great way to get moving. But group activities like playing a sport, attending a yoga class, or participating in a martial art can work even better.

What it's good for:

You'll get the same energy boosting effects from any other form of exercise, along with a social connection of being in the same room as other people, working toward a common goal.

This second benefit is *fantastic* for when we're feeling isolated, as it lets us engage with other people, but without having to carry a conversation, or do difficult, high-energy actions. The result is a feeling of less isolation, with relatively little effort.

Why it works:

We've covered the physical effects of exercise in earlier chapters, but the isolation effects are new.

Being around other people, working toward a common goal activates the parts of our brains associated with community, empathy, kindness, and well-being.

And you guessed it — all of those are super helpful in taking on depression.

How to use it:

1. Pick out a sport or group activity that you generally enjoy. If you've got a regular activity, just choose your usual.
2. When depression's in town, commit to go one time in a given week, and make it happen.
3. Make your goal just to show up, make it through, and come home — not to feel better, or do anything more than the minimums. Just showing up and physically being around other people, working toward a goal, will give you the full range of benefits.

Directly Hack Your Sympathetic and Parasympathetic Nervous Systems

What it is:

This is a neat one. Your body has two opposing systems: the sympathetic nervous system and the parasympathetic nervous system.

Despite their complicated names, they're simple in function.

Your *sympathetic* nervous system amps you up. This is the system that gets you ready to run from tigers, go skydiving, and give speeches. It increases your heart rate, dilates your pupils, and improves your hearing.

Your *parasympathetic* nervous system calms you down. This is what settles you down after stress, gets you ready to sleep, and generally makes you chill.

Both of these can be useful in dealing with your depression.

If you're really low energy, getting your sympathetic system moving is going to give you more spring in your step, and a greater ability to get things done.

If you're dealing with anxiety, your parasympathetic system can settle you down.

Happily, we can trigger both systems, easily, pretty much anywhere.

What it's good for:
Being able to quickly make adjustments to your physical state, and get your body working for you, not against you.

Why it works:

As we've looked at throughout this section, our body and physical responses can be a huge key in taking on depression, and helping our energy levels and mood.

By having two more levers you can pull to tweak your physical responses, you're even more able to steer the ship you live in.

How to use it:

Sympathetic System (Get hyped)
For your *sympathetic* system, you just need to create some stress. That can be as easy as vividly imagining yourself preparing to run an Olympic race or thinking about going skydiving. If you're in a place you can move around, you can get even better results by combining it with a minute or two of jumping jacks or shadowboxing.

Once your heart rate is up and your mind has a clear scenario, the system will kick in. You get endorphins, adrenaline, and all kinds of chemical kick-starters. It's a great way to give yourself a boost of priming energy to go take on the stuff you want.

<u>Parasympathetic System (Chill)</u>
For your *parasympathetic* system, it's as easy as breathing. Crazy as it sounds, there's a proven and ridiculously simple way to breathe that will kick your parasympathetic system into high gear, and settle you down.

It works like this:
1. Inhale through your nose, counting to four.
2. Hold your breath, counting to seven.
3. Exhale through your mouth, counting to eight.

I know. It sounds crazy. But try it right now, giving it two rounds, and tell me if you don't feel calmer. :)

Medication

What it is:

Medication. Oh boy. If there was a stigmatized part of an already stigmatized disease, this is it. Let's see if we can break all that down, and make some sense of it.

There are a handful of types of medication used to treat depression. As I'm not a doctor, I'm not even going to attempt to describe them, their effects, or their side effects.

Suffice to say that they've all been clinically shown to have some positive effect in treating depression, and they all have some side effects that vary from person to person — just like any other medicine.

Medications that treat depression aren't available without a prescription in most countries, so you'd need to see a doctor if you wanted to try this tool out.

But let's dig into why you might want to, in the first place.

What it's good for:

Here's what medication can do: *it can give you more spoons.*

That's it. It won't make you magically depression free, it won't change the structure of your brain that's causing your depression, and it won't turn you into some artificially buoyant happykin, floating through their life.

But for many folks, the ability to have a few more spoons in the rough times of depression means they're able to take other actions (like the ones this book is full of) that they wouldn't have energy to otherwise.

If you can view medication as something that can give you a little more energy, it becomes a tool you can make an informed decision on, and decide if any risks or side effects are worth it.

But I want to put out one word of warning: If you go to your regular doctor (not a mental health professional), it's possible they won't actually understand that distinction, nor really what depression is about.

Many general practice doctors prescribe anti-depressants as a "cure" that will fix depression all on their own, simply because they don't know better. You do.

If you're interested in adding medication to your toolbox, go to a psychiatrist or prescribing mental health nurse for the prescription. They're the experts.

Overall, if medication seems helpful to you, get it! Just don't neglect everything else. :)

Why it works:

The mechanism varies between medication, but they're all tweaking your brain chemistry and hormones to reduce your symptoms. These tweaks are also where the side effects can come from, and they vary (as you might expect) from person to person as our bodies and brain chemistry varies.

But broadly, on the population as a whole, they've been shown to help out.

How to use it:

To me, really using medication effectively comes down to viewing it as *one tool* in your toolbox, instead of a magic-bullet solution.

Many people who deal with depression find medication to be tremendously helpful in finding more energy and being able to do other things that help them out and let them pursue lives they love.

Some folks who deal with depression find that the interactions between their bodies and the meds create side effects that don't justify the extra spoons.

And a few people who deal with depression and only use medication find that when they stop taking the medication, their depression returns. This makes sense — they haven't built any of the other supports, or created a well-rounded response to their depression. Don't let this be you.

Medication can help give you more energy and more spoons. But make sure — if you choose to use it — it's only one part of your well-developed, well-rounded toolbox.

A technique if you're worried about side effects:

Work with a doctor to try things out for a defined period of time, and take notes, as follows.

1. For a few days before you start the medication, jot down how you feel, your mood, and any side effects, every day in a journal.

2. Then, after a few days of notes, try the medication for 3 weeks, keep taking notes, and see what happens.

3. After three weeks, review your notes, see what's happening, and decide if you like it or not.

4. Whether you decide to go off the medication or stay on, work with your doctor to do it safely — some medications can have serious side effects if they're stopped too abruptly.

The decision — and the responsibility — rests with you. Do what's best for yourself.

You've now got some great tools to use your body to take on depression. Next up, let's take a step outside ourselves and look at some set-and-forget tools: your environment.

YOUR ENVIRO NMENT

Introduction

So far, we've focused on things you can do, and using your mind and body to directly take on your depression.

But one of the things that makes us special as human beings is our capacity to change the world around us. And it turns out investing a little energy into shifting our environment can have a huge impact in taking on our depression.

Environmental changes are some of my favorites, because they're set-and-forget. We simply make the change, then let the better environment influence us every day.

Let's dig into some good ones.

Get More Light

What it is:

Yep, light.

I don't mean this in a metaphorical, "go toward the light" kind of way. I mean physically get more bright bunches of photons hitting your retinas and skin.

There's a lot of research on the effect of light deprivation on mood, and a variety of depression-like symptoms. There's even a name with a nifty acronym for the collection — Seasonal Affective Disorder (SAD).

Yeah. They named it SAD.

Anyhow, SAD tends to look a lot like depression and often runs alongside it. In practice, it's something that can pile on and make a depressive episode a lot worse.

SAD tends to hit the hardest in the winter months and is worse the further from the equator you live.

To combat it, you simply get more light. If you live somewhere with ample sunlight and you've been living in a windowless basement, just go outside and spend some time there.

If you don't, this means adding more light in your home (and office, if you can manage), and paying attention to light intensity, timing, and color.

What it's good for:

Bringing up your mood, getting you some Vitamin D, and reducing any pile-on effects from SAD that might be making your depression worse.

Why it works:

Light is deeply tied to all sorts of chemicals and reactions in our brains and bodies. Our serotonin levels, cortisol, and all the myriad chemicals that tell us when it's time to sleep and when it's time to wake up and be engaged are directly affected by the intensity (and color) of light we see.

In our modern lives, it's easy to forget that we're basically creatures who have lived under the sun in temperate climates for years and years and years.

But our bodies haven't forgotten the sun, and it still has a big impact on our lives.

How to use it:

If you're somewhere that has good amounts of sun, open up your windows, and get outside for a little bit every day. The earlier in your day you can get sunlight hitting your retinas, the better.

If you live in a dark and rainy part of the world, investing in and learning to use some lights specifically proven to help with SAD can make a big difference. (I lived in rainy Portland, Oregon in the United States for a number of years and having good lights made a massive impact.)

There are also smart lights these days that can change color and mimic a 12-hour day. Bluish in the morning, yellowish at night. These too, can have a big effect.

Move All Your Furniture

What it is:

Move all the furniture in your house around. Change everything.

What it's good for:

Breaking up habitual patterns and bringing us into the present moment.

It's also great for establishing new ways you want to relax, unwind, or deal with times you're low on energy.

Why it works:

As we looked at in previous sections, one of the best things we can do to combat depression is to bring our attention into the present moment, and out of our thoughts.

When we change our environments dramatically, all the habits we have for moving through a space (as well as where we go and what we do when we're low on energy) are thrown off.

With that disruption, we have a blank slate to create new patterns for our lives that we like better, and we're forced to pay attention to what's around us (or we'll bump our shins on the table!)

How to use it:

Take an afternoon, and commit to just moving every single piece of furniture in your house, even slightly. Rearrange your bathroom, and move your toothbrush to a new location. Your goal is to make the space you live in feel new and unfamiliar.

Then, as you move through this new space, put some intention into how you'd like to interact with it. Where would you like to unwind, and what would that look like?

Where would you like to go when you're out of energy, and what do you want to do? What's the first thing you want to do in the morning?

Let yourself create new patterns you love, and then try them out and see how they work.

Wear Different Clothes

What it is:

Wear completely different clothes. If you're usually dressed up, dress down for a bit. If you're usually relaxed, try dressing up.

What it's good for:

Shaking up your sense of self, and opening up new opportunities for how you can interact with the world.

It's also great for getting us out of ruts.

Why it works:

Clothing and grooming also play key roles in our identity — the stories we tell about ourselves. By changing these up, we're able to ask new questions about ourselves, and find new ways of answering them.

How would someone wearing formalwear choose to unwind and spend their evenings? Probably differently than someone in sweatpants and a comfy cardigan. Changing up our look gives us new options for being and interacting.

How to use it:

Pick one day that you'd like to experiment with a new look, and go all out. Dress the part, and style your hair and face to match.

Then, dressed in your new style, see what seems like an interesting way to spend your time. Notice if there are new things you'd be interested in doing, and if so, engage with them.

Often, a new set of clothes prompts a new set of things we could do. Follow those instincts, and see where they lead you.

Stop Drinking

What it is:

Yep, I said it.

I love a craft beer or a nice cocktail or glass of wine as much (or maybe more) than the next person. But when I notice depression coming to town, I know it's time to take a break.

What it's good for:

Keeping your energy level up, and encouraging you to eat.

Why it works:

The main reason is one you've heard before — alcohol is a depressant.

This doesn't mean that alcohol magically *gives* you depression, it just means that it piles on top of your existing depression, and makes it *worse*.

Think of alcohol as taking away half your spoons every morning. That 20% energy level drops to 10%, right off the bat. Don't like that idea? Don't give it your spoons.

Worse, alcohol is often tied to habits where a couple drinks turns into a dozen. Besides sapping your energy, this also throws a ton of carbs and sugars at your digestive system, which it generally responds to by getting sleepy and putting you to bed.

It also adds a bunch of empty calories, which means instead of feeding your hunger with the nutrients and minerals your brain needs to work properly, your body has to run on pure sugar, and suck vitamins out of other parts of itself. Not good.

It's true that often, alcohol will dull the sadness that comes with depression — but it will also exacerbate the cause.

If you can avoid alcohol when depression is in town, your depression will leave more quickly, you'll have more energy, and the experience will overall be less severe.

How to use it:

The simplest and easiest way to avoid alcohol when depression is in town is just to get it out of the house.

Your support person can be a big help here. Let's say you've got a nice bottle of whiskey or some excellent wine you enjoy. That's great.

When you notice that Aunt Dee's shown up, just ask your support person to take the bottles over to their house for a little while.

Aunt Dee turns out to be a voracious drinker, and given the chance, she'll gulp down all your fine whiskey in a slurred, cheeto-laced bender. Worse, she won't appreciate it, and she won't share.

Your whiskey deserves better, and so do you.

You can also try just to avoid drinking, but I'm not going to lie — it's not easy. When you're down and out of spoons, having a drink often seems like a *great* idea. And when you're out of energy, you're not going to have the willpower to say no.

This is why — however you can manage it — while depression is in town, get the alcohol out of the house. When it's passed, it'll still be there for you to fully and properly enjoy, without having to share it with Aunt Dee.

Stop Smoking Weed

What it is:

I can feel the haters already, but it's true.

Like alcohol, weed is a depressant on your system, and it's generally going to make the experience worse, and last longer.

What it's good for:

Keeping your energy level up, and encouraging you to eat healthy.

Why it works:

The same things we talked about in the last chapter also apply here.

Weed being a depressant doesn't mean it magically *gives* you depression, it just means that it piles on top of your existing depression, and makes it *worse*.

And, like alcohol (though itself not as bad), weed is tied to eating habits that aren't super helpful. An entire tray of brownies won't help you feel any better in the morning, and it won't help your brain run more smoothly.

If you can avoid weed when depression is in town, your depression will generally leave more quickly, you'll have more energy, and the overall experience will be less severe.

How to use it:

Just like alcohol, the simplest and easiest way to avoid weed when depression is in town is just to get it out of the house.

If you have a friend who doesn't smoke, tell them you're taking a break for a little while, and ask if they'd be willing to keep an eye on it.

Just like alcohol, Aunt Dee will also smoke your entire stash, make you go buy more, and hot-box your apartment in a haze that you won't even remember going by. While staining your couch with cheeto-fingers. *Dammit, Aunt Dee.*

Your weed deserves better, and so do you.

Same advice as alcohol applies here — you can also try just to keep your weed in the house and avoid smoking, but it's not easy.

When you're down and out of spoons, having a smoke to unwind can seems like a *great* idea. And when you're out of energy, you're not going to have the willpower to say no.

This is why — however you can manage it — while depression is in town, get your stash out of the house. When it's passed, it'll still be there for you to fully and properly enjoy, without having to share it with Aunt Dee.

Move To a New City

What it is:

Pack up all your stuff, and move somewhere new.

Holy extreme options, Batman!

I know. It *is* extreme. But it also might help, and if you can do it, it's not a bad thing to try out.

What it's good for:

Bringing up your mood (via the get more light) strategy, breaking up unhealthy habits, and getting you away from painful memories.

Especially if you're affected by sunlight and you live somewhere that tends toward the dark and grey, moving to a sunnier locale can do wonders in taking on your depression.

Additionally, if your current city is tied to lots of sad memories, traumatic experiences, or triggers, moving will literally get them out of your life.

"Wherever you go, there you are" is true. But also true is "Wherever you go, your ex's new boyfriend will generally stay behind."

Why it works:

A change of scenery can allow us to step into new facets of who we are, and leave behind parts we don't want. Anyone who's moved away for college or a job has experienced this sense of forming a new identity, and if there are parts of your current life that exacerbate your depression, you can literally leave them behind.

The second reason is light and weather. If your sort of depression is affected by light and you live in a dark, rainy city, moving to somewhere tropical with lots of light is worth serious thought.

This is actually why I live all over the world, in mostly tropical climates. In rainy Portland, I learned that light has a huge impact on my mood and exacerbates my depression, so I decided that whatever it took, I wasn't going to live anywhere dark ever again.

Finally, examining or deciding to move can also give us a burst of energy, and something to focus on and engage with. That in itself is tremendous in taking on depression and can make a difference.

How to use it:

1. Take some time and think about what you're looking for in a new city, and what you want to leave behind.

2. Make a list of cities that have what you're looking for: more light, access to the beach, hiking. Whatever things will make your day-to-day experience better.

3. Look into logistics. This is the stuff like where you'd live, what you'd do for work, and how you'd meet new people once you'd moved there. Make sure to have

answers to all three of those questions (too many folks skip the third one)!

4.   With that holistic view, ask yourself if this move is something you want to try. Moving is something that often gets built up into something bigger than it really is. View your move as an experiment. If you like it, you can stay there. If you hate it, you can move back. The consequences for "getting it wrong" are much smaller in reality than our imaginations.

5.   If you want to give it a shot, pack yourself up and make the move! See what kind of life is waiting on the other side.

Go on Vacation

What it is:

Is moving to a new city too extreme? Cool. Just go on a vacation.

Picking somewhere sunny is generally a good idea, as is picking somewhere new.

What it's good for:

Upping your mood, disrupting habits, and getting yourself plenty of sunlight — all the same stuff as moving to a new city, with none of the big-life changes.

Why it works:

The sun will give you light to improve your mood, and Vitamin D.

The new place will mean you've got no cues or triggers in the environment, and can shake up your routines and habits enough that your depression may get shaken hard, too.

Vacations are a great place to try out new routines for a day, new ways of thinking about yourself, and of course, a great place to recharge and get away from all the energy-sucking expectations of the world.

How to use it:

Find somewhere sunny and warm, find where you'd like to go, and save up some money to pay for the trip when the time comes.

Then, when Aunt Dee comes to town, toss her the house keys, and tell her you'll be back. Casually mention you're out of cheetos. Then get on a plane to Barbados. :)

Super-Schedule Your Day

What it is:

Make a super-detailed schedule for your day, and follow it.

What it's good for:

This one isn't for everyone, and even for those of us for whom it works well, it's not an all the time thing. But it can really work.

Taking some time to super-schedule out your day ends up reducing your choices (and the decision fatigue they cause), and lets you save your spoons for actually doing things.

When you're super, super low on energy, consider making a strong schedule, and then letting yourself follow it. It can make those tough days a lot easier.

Why it works:

We think of energy as something we spend *doing* things. But it's also spent every time we make a decision.

In a normal day, those decisions are pretty small fry, and they don't take a lot out of us. But on the bad days with depression when we're running on 5% or less of our normal energy, those little decisions start to have a big toll.

By creating a schedule and plan for our day, we get rid of all our decisions, and are able to save our energy for actually engaging in activities.

It might seem claustrophobic or overbearing when you have lots of energy, but in those really low places, it's actually a tremendous relief.

How to use it:

1. Write out an hour-by-hour grid for your day, or your week.

2. Fill in each hour with what you want to spend it doing. Pay attention to your energy level, and be honest. Schedule yourself days that are achievable and will really work.

    As you schedule your day, be intentional about putting things in your schedule that will get you more energy, and note which things are likely to drain your reserves. This is your chance to be tactical. Take it.

3. If, like me, you sometimes lose track of time, set up an hour chime on your phone or watch, so you note the hours passing.

4. That's it. When you wake up, just grab your schedule, and follow along.

You've now got some great ways to change your environment, and take on your depression. But how do you catch it early, and notice it's shown up? With these next tools, specifically for noticing depression.

TOOLS TO NOTICE DEPRE SSION

AWESOME TOOLS TO DEAL WITH DEPRESSION

Introduction

You now have some great tools to take on depression when it comes to town. But that relies on one critical thing — knowing it's there.

Since depression changes the very way we see the world, this can be tricker than it might seem at first glance. In this section, we'll take a look at some tools to help you notice that Aunt Dee's sitting on the couch and that it's time to grab your toolbox.

"Red Flag" Thoughts, Words, and Patterns

As you live with depression, you'll learn to spot (and you probably already know a few already) "red flag" thoughts, words, and patterns that can let you know Aunt Dee is in town.

Learning to notice and identify these red flags early can really help you in taking on your depression by letting you catch it —and act on it — early.

Red flags can be anything — things you find yourself thinking, saying, or doing.

Here are some of mine:

- Thoughts of worthlessness
- Thoughts of self harm
- General, recurring "beating myself up" kinds of thoughts
- Getting less done than normal for no apparent reason
- Craving alcohol
- Craving sweets
- Finding myself watching lots more TV or playing more video games than normal

Some of these things in and of themselves don't mean that Aunt Dee is in town. But they're associated with her frequently enough that when I see them, I know it's time for me to stop, look around, and see what's happening.

Let's find and set up some red flags for you.

Right now, make a list of the red flags you know about in your toolbox.

Once you've got a list, jot down the following three questions on the same page. Any time that you notice one of your red flags, ask yourself these three questions:

1. How has my energy level been the last few days?
2. Have I seen any of my other red flags?
3. Does it seem like I'm experiencing depression right now? If so, what kind of day with depression is it?

It's possible that you'll answer with "pretty good", "nope", and "nah, not really." It's also possible that you'll notice Aunt Dee, sitting on the corner of your couch, whispering.

Either way, you're fine. You've noticed where you are, and you've got the tools to deal with it.

Know Your Triggers

Like our "red flag" thoughts, words, and actions, it's also important for us to get to know things that often trigger our depression — or as I like to think of it — jackass things that call Aunt Dee and give her our new address.

These triggers are deeply personal, and they're tied to our experiences, often to earlier times that we experienced depression.

But by knowing what they are, you'll sometimes be able to see depression coming, plan for it, take action, and more times than not, make it just a passing storm.

Here are some of the things on my list of triggers:

- Time with my parents
- Prolonged grey, rainy days without sun
- Fort Minor's "The Rising Tied" album
- Remembering previous really hard places in previous depressions
- Thinking about and talking about depression a lot (say, while writing this very book)
- Breakups, relationship ends, losses of friendship
- Being hungry
- Being tight on money
- Christmas

Those things aren't kryptonite — they don't immediately undo me or turn me into a blubbering mass — but they *do* make it more likely that depression is going to come calling, and if it's here, more likely that I'll go into the bad or really bad days.

Knowing that lets me make big, long-term priorities with my life, to sail around the trouble spots. This isn't a weakness. Just like if we were sailing a boat, it'd be foolish to just cut a line through storms and eddies we could clearly see coming. Taking a similar tack on our depression is a wise way to steer.

And when we know we have no other choice but to sail through the storm (as I mentioned, like my process of writing this book, or the holidays for many people) we can plan ahead and take precautions.

Before I started writing, I contacted all my support people, put my plans for weight loss on hold, moved somewhere sunny, and made sure my finances were in good shape. And overall, though depression has been here throughout the book-writing process, it's been manageable.

Just like a ship, there's a lot we can do to make sure we successfully ride out a storm.

Beware the Fruitcake

There's one particular trigger deserves special mention because of its widespread impact: the dark days of late Fall and Winter.

Those days mean holidays, more time indoors, less light and a pile of unhelpful contributors.

And they mean fruitcake.

And who likes fruitcake? Aunt Dee likes fruitcake. Of course she does. So she visits *everyone she can.*

It's kind of mind-blowing, but every winter, I see the traffic to my articles on depression go up more than *ten thousand percent.* Clearly, it's a tough time for us all.

In the Northern hemisphere, the rough spot seems to start right about the middle of November, and carry on through the new year. In the South, things kick off around mid-June.

For so many of us, those few months are the most difficult of the entire year.

The reasons are varied. For a lot of us, holidays come with family, and family is an inextricable part of our journey with depression. They're often the people who were around when we first experienced it, and as we'll talk about in the next section, they often give some of the most well-meaning responses to depression that are also the least helpful.

It's also colder, a lot of activities we love aren't available, and the days are short and dark.

It's totally possible the winter and holidays won't be a big deal for you. But I'd keep an eye on them just in case.

And if you're one of us for whom the winter and holidays can be a mess of happy and awful — know that you're not alone, and feel free to plan ahead.

Whatever and however you choose to engage in those times, all of us — the millions and millions of us who deal with depression — have your back.

Monthly Check-In

One of the clients I coached also dealt with depression from time to time, and on each of our calls, I always made sure to ask, "How is your depression?".

It felt like a strange question to ask — after all, if their depression was doing well, wouldn't I be kind of a jerk for bringing it up?

But the reality was the opposite. By asking that question consistently, we created a baseline grounded in experience — that most of the time, the answer was "Great. I'm not experiencing depression at all."

When it did show up, it wasn't alone, or isolated as a singular event, but a blip on a very large timeline — like it often is, in our day-to-day lives.

Having a regular check-in is great for getting a sense of perspective on where you are, how often depression really shows up, *and* for catching it when it sneaks in the back door.

It's also super easy to do. Just put a recurring reminder on your calendar (on the same day each month,) and put the following questions in it:

1. How has my energy level been the last month?
2. Have I seen any of my red flags?
3. Does it seem like I've been experiencing depression this month? How about right now? If so, what kind of day with depression is it?

I actually keep a record of these questions, by jotting them down in a notebook — it lets me look back and know that my depression typically stops by 2-3 times a year, usually doesn't go past the bad days, and in all, is around for about a month and a half out of each year.

That lets me plan, understand, and most of all, have inarguable facts when depression does stop by that it *will* in fact leave, in time.

If you're the kind of person who finds that comforting, you might like keeping a record too!

Morning Check-in

To get a more frequent view of how you're doing, consider a morning check-in.

When you wake up, first thing in the morning, just notice how you're feeling that day.

Do you feel like you have all your spoons? If not, how many are missing? What percentage is your energy level at?

Are there Crazy Thoughts?

Do a quick check-in, and see where you find yourself, first thing in the morning.

Doing this will let you plan your day and be aware if you'll need to be mindful about where you spend your spoons.

A quick morning check-in is an essential habit when depression is in town, but it's also a lovely one to keep going even when Aunt Dee's taken off. Just like the monthly check-in, it can give us a sense of perspective and understanding about the rhythms of our lives.

As you're setting one up, definitely consider pairing it with the mindfulness tool we talked about back on page 101. They go great together.

Sometimes, Depression Will Sneak In Anyway

It seems like if we know we have depression, we understand our red flags, and we have the tools to handle it, that we'll always be able to fend it off successfully, and make sure it never comes back.

But it doesn't always work that way — because depression distorts how we see the world.

Let me tell you a quick story about a recent visit I had from depression.

A few weeks after I moved to Thailand, I noticed that I was feeling off. I was grumpy and wanting to quit my day job (more than normal), getting like 10% of the things I usually get done completed, and spending most of my time sitting on the couch, playing video games.

I like video games. But I rarely play them for more than a few minutes a day, to unwind. This was hours a day, every day, eating into everything else I did.

But it never crossed my mind that I might be experiencing depression. I just thought my job sucked and life had always been sort of grey and that video games were a real and totally normal connection with feeling and life.

After one business call, walking to my bedroom, I was muttering to myself, and caught myself about to say, *"I wish I could just die."*

That moment — for the first time in almost ten days of what was pretty clearly depression — was the first time I realized Aunt Dee was in town.

I wrote a fucking book on this stuff, and I still didn't catch her when she'd snuck in late one weekend night almost two weeks past.

Sometimes, depression is sneaky like this.

It'll worm its way into your life, without you knowing. Because the first thing it does is affect our view of reality, it's really hard to notice without any kind of external reference.

When this happens, all we can do is notice it whenever we notice, and then take action.

I told my support people. And I got really fucking pissed. I said some *very* blue words to Aunt Dee, and told her what I thought. The fuck if she got to barge into one of my favorite cities in the world, drain all the color out, and schlup me down on the couch like some kind of sea sludge. Fuck that, and fuck her.

I ordered some Thai food (pizza in Bangkok is pretty sketchy), pulled out my Behavioral Activation tool, and got moving.

And I took on Aunt Dee, Steven's Bad-Ass Toolbox of Depression Conquering in hand.

A week later, she was gone. Sometimes, this will happen to you too. It's totally normal and totally ok. Just kick her sorry ass off the couch when you notice her.

You're now fully equipped with ways to notice when depression has shown up, and a variety of tools for your mind, body, actions, and environment. We've got one more type of tool left, and they're for a super-specific situation: tools for the deep dark places.

TOOLS FOR THE DEEP DARK PLACES

Tools for Handling the Deep Dark Places

The deep dark places are the scariest and deadliest parts of depression.

Surviving them when they come requires tools all their own. But it also requires an attitude.

In this section, we'll dig into both, and make sure you get out of the deep dark places alive and healthy.

Treat It Like Drunk Driving

When you're in the bad, really bad, or "false well" days, treat your depression like drunk driving. Trust one of your support people to be your eyes and ears and to make sure you get home safely.

Like drunk driving, in these places, our minds and narratives of the world aren't reliable.

How many drunk drivers thought, "Sure, I'm fine to drive," before getting into the car? Almost all of them.

The same goes for your depression. If you're in one of the worse days, you may have Crazy Thoughts that will seem normal, and find yourself thinking stuff like, "Sure, jumping in front of a train seems reasonable. I'm coherent enough — the world is just really fucked up and nobody loves me."

But just like drunk driving, your judgement is impaired.

Run these thoughts by the support people you trust. If they say, "Eh, I mean, the world's kind of shitty, but that sounds like a crazy thought to me," *it's a crazy thought.* Trust them.

Yes, this entire disease is serious bullshit.

But it can also be deadly. Trusting our support people to be our reliable eyes and ears is one of the best ways we can make it through the scary parts.

Treat It Like Severe Allergies

You know what people with peanut allergies don't fuck around with? Peanuts.

The reason is simple and obvious — peanuts can kill them in a matter of minutes. That's why they become obsessive about reading ingredients, and carry around emergency injectors in case something sneaks in.

Your depression can also kill you.

So treat it with that same intention. Don't fuck around with it. Get support people. Figure out how it works. Make plans around dealing with it in worst-case scenarios, and never let up on it.

We can live full, wonderful lives with depression. But we have to stay vigilant.

This encompasses all aspects of our lives — environment included.

People with peanut allergies don't keep jars of peanut butter in the house. Treat your depression the same way.

If you get severe depression, don't own a gun, and don't keep bottles of pills around. Make it as difficult as possible for you to commit suicide. Remember, you won't have much energy at the low parts, and you can use that to your advantage in the worst parts by making really shitty things really hard to do.

Make living the easy choice.

Act Preemptively

This is a *big* one. Because our judgement is one of the first things to go, we need to act sooner than we think we should.

This means reaching out to support people when depression has just started to pop up, so they know to be on the lookout for it taking a dive.

It means if you've had one crazy thought, even if you could identify it and note that it was a crazy thought, *tell all your support people.*

Could it be nothing? Of course. But if that bout of depression does happen to get worse, your judgement will go, and go fast.

We put a lot of effort into getting, training, and building trust with our support people. They know what to expect, and they know it could all be a flash in the pan. They're also people who aren't going to freak out or get super worried, because they understand how this works.

Tell them. Sooner than you think is necessary.

To make it as easy as possible, right in your bad-ass depression fighting toolbox, make a list of what to do if you have a crazy thought, and give yourself all the steps:

- A list of people
- Their contact info
- A script on what to tell them

Make it as easy as possible for you to take care of yourself.

Make a Plan When You're Not Depressed

The drunk-driving metaphor holds here too.

The best time to make a plan to get home after a night of drinking is before you go out, while you're sober.

The same's true for your depression. The best time to make a plan, get support people, and build the resources you need is when you're not in the middle of a visit from depression.

Sometimes, that's the only option, and that's fine. If Aunt Dee's in town for you right now, just do the best you can do in setting up and getting support right now.

But later, when she's left, go back and review your toolbox, end-to-end. Reach out and re-evaluate your support people. Do a little bit of work while you're in a good place, and it'll save you tons and tons of effort (and make your life much easier) on depression's next visit.

Don't Be Afraid to Call the Pros

This is an obvious one, but still worth mentioning because it can be really helpful.

The Pros have trained their whole lives to be able to help in situations like these. Leverage them if you can.

We'll talk more about them in the next section, but pros can also be really useful just as consultants.

Review your plan and support structure with them, and see if there are any blind spots you've missed.

A lot of times, we think of mental health professionals as being a last line of defense, laying us back on a couch and probing all our deepest childhood traumas.

But they're better — lots better — as collaborators. If you can, bring 'em in when you're planning and get their opinions. They're experts for a reason.

Know Your Warning Signs

Alright. Now we're getting tactical. Warning signs are things you or one of your support people can notice that indicate you're in a bad, really bad, or "false well" day, that mean support goes into active mode.

These can be things like:

- Having a suicidal thought
- Having a thought about self harm or harming others
- Finding yourself massively pessimistic about the world
- Expressing that your life has no value

Make a list for yourself, and share it with your support people. If one of these happens, no matter what, just let them know.

Make Binding Agreements with Your Support People

Remember that "Take it seriously" commitment you made back in *The Pledge*? Yeah, we're leaning on that again.

Make binding agreements with your support people to do whatever they think is needed to help you out in a critical situation. Give them keys to your house, the contact information for any professionals you're working with, your insurance information, the whole nine yards.

Get specific. Things like if you're in a really bad day, and you haven't responded to a check-in in 24 hours, that they can come on over to your house and see how you're doing.

I know. That sounds scary as fuck.

But actually, what it's doing is the opposite. It's setting up a system where you know that no matter what, someone is looking out for you.

Will your support person ever come charging into your house with ice cream and a look of serious concern? No, probably not.

But knowing they *could* will help you stay honest in communicating with them, and it'll help them feel better in trusting you in those dark places.

If you had a serious medical condition like a weak heart or diabetes, you'd do the same thing.

Depression can kill you.

Give the people around you the best shot of saving you, if it ever got that bad.

When You're In the Deep Dark Place: Focus on Surviving

When you're in a really dark place, spend your spoons and energy on two things, and two things only:

- De-powering harmful thoughts, and
- Getting more spoons.

That's it.

Let's look at each in a little more detail.

De-powering harmful thoughts.

On the worst days, self-harming, dark thoughts come with the territory for a lot of us. In those times, your goal is to focus on getting distance and perspective on your thoughts, and deflating their power.

We've covered a lot of tools that can help in shifting your relationship to your thoughts, and noticing and handling thoughts as they come by.

In the deep dark places, it's time to really lean on those tools.

While the thoughts that we get in the deep dark places can be intense, disturbing, and dangerous, critically — they are **still just thoughts**, like all the other ones we experience.

On these days, focus on keeping that perspective, and be vigilant on identifying those thoughts as *thoughts*.

That simple identification really helps, because it gives us perspective, and that perspective deflates the thoughts of much of their power.

Just like if I had a thought one afternoon about riding a unicycle around my neighborhood naked while singing the collected works of *Mott the Hoople*, just *having the thought* doesn't mean I have to *act on it*. Same goes for the thoughts we get in the deep dark places. They're just thoughts. We still control our actions.

To put it in practice, pick one or two of your favorite thought-focused tools, and use them, every day, until you're through the bad days (and the weird "false well" days). Here's a quick reminder of some tools we've covered:

- Talk to your support person
- Write
- Journal
- Mindfulness
- Talk to yourself, your dog, your plants, or a rubber duckie
- Present moment awareness
- Rephrase it

Go with whatever tools make it easy for you to get perspective on your thoughts, and power them down.

Getting more spoons.

Most of the tools in this book are about getting more energy. Pick your favorite few, and use them. Order pizza. Get a workout in. Start a creative project. Take a cold shower, and slather everything with hot sauce.

If you can, choose tools that also let you get out of your thoughts, and focus on something external.

But when you're picking how to spend the limited energy you have, focus — exclusively — on getting more spoons.

That wraps up the tools you'll need to handle the deep dark places. Before we move on, let's take a quick step back.

You Have the Tools

Whew! That's all of the tools.

We've gone through more than 60 tools in this section, covering everything from awesome mental frames to weird body hacks (I'm betting you weren't expecting to find "Eat Spicy Food" in this book!).

You have tools to handle everything from the good days to the deep dark places.

Now it's time to make them your own.

Look at this section as a big tool bin you can rummage through from time to time, try things out, and see what works for you.

Build your toolbox, and stack it full of your favorites — things that feel comfortable in your hands, and that really work for you and your experience of depression.

Just like that wonderful house with troublesome plumbing we talked about in the beginning, you'll find yourself with a great toolbox and able to handle whatever comes your way sooner than you'd think.

One last piece of advice: every once in a while, maybe every year or two, come on back and flip through these tools again.

See if there are tools that didn't resonate before that do now, or things that used to work that you'd like to drop.

It's your bad-ass depression-fighting toolbox. Make it one you love, and keep it current as you and your life grows and changes.

Alright, so you've got tools to handle depression when it stops by. But what about everyone around us, and what's the deal with these awesome support people I keep mentioning?

Let's dive into the next section — all about the people in our lives.

PEOPLE

Introduction

People. They're simultaneously the most helpful and most difficult part of dealing with a visit from depression.

In this section, we're going to break down all the different types of people you may find in your life, and give you the tools to handle each of them.

Here's the how we group them, in this book:

- Your Support People
- Anti-Support people
- Family and Friends
- Coworkers and Classmates, Teachers and Bosses
- Everyone Else
- The Pros

As we talked about way back in the beginning in "Relationships Get Weird" (p 61), there's a difference between how close someone might be and how helpful they are to have around when you're dealing with a visit from Aunt Dee.

In this section, we'll approach people from the perspective of what's most helpful to you in dealing with depression.

Note that this doesn't mean that we're ignoring those close relationships that don't happen to be super helpful — we just know those people will still be there once Aunt Dee has left town.

Let's get started with the best of the best — your awesome support people.

About Awesome Support People

Awesome support people are fantastic. They effectively give us support, don't take any energy, and they understand what's going on.

They know how to check in, how to listen — even to the crazy stuff — and we can count on them to be there and to help get us through.

Weirdly though, they're not always the people closest to us.

That strange truth is because awesome support people **must** have these two qualities:

1. They care about us.
2. They're capable of looking at their reactions, understanding, and changing.

Not everybody has both of those, and that's ok. Not having both doesn't mean someone's not a great person — but it does mean they're not going to be a great *support* person.

However, the folks in your life who do have both qualities can make amazing supports, and give you a tool unlike anything else in dealing with depression.

We'll walk through finding and preparing your support folks, but to whet your appetite, once you've got your people, getting support will be as simple as having a quick conversation or text exchange that goes like this:

> *You:* Hey, Bill. Aunt Dee's in town.
>
> *Bill:* Ugh. Fucking Aunt Dee! That sucks. Don't worry, I've got your back.
>
> *You:* Yeah. Total bullshit.
>
> *Bill:* How are you doing today?
>
> *You:* I'm doing ok right now - it's a good day - but I wanted to reach out and let you know as we agreed.
>
> *Bill:* For sure. Thank you for doing it. I'm going to keep checking in with you like we talked about until she takes off. :)
>
> *You:* Thanks.
>
> *Bill:* You got it. Don't forget to order a pizza.
>
> *You:* Oh man, I forgot! Ordering right now.

And that's it.

This quick conversation tells Bill that depression is coming for a visit. Since you've already talked to Bill about what that means and what to expect, he's now planning to check in with you.

He'll be there to help get anything out of your head, take a load off, and generally help shoulder the burden of Aunt Dee — with no judgement, and no weirdness.

Sounds pretty great, right? It is.

Let's dig into how to get awesome support people, how to train them, and everything you need to know to build an effective support network.

How to Get Awesome Support People

Alright, so awesome support people sound pretty great. But how do you find them? Well, as I mentioned, your support people need to have two different qualities.

1. They care about us.
2. They're capable of looking at their reactions, understanding, and changing.

So let's start there.

First, make a list of all the people you know who are capable of looking at their behavior and consciously changing their actions. Be honest, and fair.

Come back here when you're done.

Got a list? Great.

Next, make a list of all the people you know who care about you. As a reference, you can ask this question when you think about people. "If I told _____ I was dealing with depression, would they want to help?" Be honest, and if it's close, err on the side of "yes." People tend to care a lot more than we think.

Come on back when you're done.

Got it? Tremendous.

Finally, make one last list of the people who show up on both lists.

These are your potential support people.

Put them in order of who you'd *like* to be a support person, and before you turn to the next chapter, reach out to three of them. Here's a sample of how to do it.

> Hey Jillian,
>
> So, as you know, I deal with depression from time to time, and I've recently decided to get serious about it and start really taking care of myself.
>
> In that process, I'm picking a few people out to act as "support people" — folks I can talk to when depression's in town, and who would be willing to check in on me periodically when I've told you I'm getting a visit from depression.
>
> I'd let you know what to expect, and what I'd need, and you'd also have the contact information for my other support folks.
>
> Is this something you'd be willing and have the energy to do on occasion?
>
> Thanks so much!

Once you've got a few people, give them each other's contact info, and then dig into and share the next sections, on helping them know what to do!

How Many Support People Do You Need?

3-5 is the short answer.

The long answer is it depends.

What you're looking for is the right number of people so that:
- You have someone you can call when you need it,
- You're not overwhelmed by the check-ins,
- Your support people aren't overwhelmed by the support work,
- It's easy for you to get the support ball rolling, and
- You don't get lost between too many people.

The right number will depend on what kind of days you're having. On the really bad and false well days, you're going to want a *lot* of support. On the good days, you'll only need a little.

But you'll want to have enough support people that when you need more help, you know it's there.

You'll also want to consider the emotional labor your support people are doing, and spread the load around. It's tempting and really easy to get one super-awesome support person and to just lean on them when you need help.

This will work, and it's better than nothing. But it will also take a toll on your relationship, and you run a risk if that person's on vacation in Antarctica. Having a few support people will give you the best of both worlds — a close community and consistent support, and it will keep all your relationships in great shape.

Feeling Iffy on Actually Reaching Out?

That's totally normal.

For most of us, the idea of reaching out and setting up support relationships feels scary and terribly vulnerable. If you feel this way, you're definitely not alone.

One of the stories depression likes to tell about itself is how shameful it is, and how we shouldn't tell anyone, or people will look down on us. *That story is complete and utter bullshit.*

When I first reached out to my support people, it was super scary. But folks generally said yes, and everyone was hugely supportive.

But I found out something funny in the process — they were more nervous than me! They really wanted to help, but were worried that they didn't really know what to do. Once I shared the stuff in the next section with them, and we got our big conversation out of the way, everyone felt comfortable.

At the end, instead of shame or anxiety, what I felt most — was *relief.*

Having a few great support people is one of the biggest pillars to making sure your depression is well-managed in the long-term, and only plays a small part in your life.

Remember way back at the start, when you said out loud, "I'm willing to do some difficult things"? Getting started on this part might be one of them.

But I promise, it'll be worth it, and worth spending the energy to get the ball rolling.

C'mon. Let's build some effective support around us, and take some of the load off.

Reach out to three folks off your list if you haven't already, then let's dive into how to give them they tools they'll need!

How to Train Your Awesome Support People

Wait, train? But they're supposed to be wonderful, caring people who can change their behavior!

They are.

But they probably don't know *noodles* about how to help out with depression, and even less about your particular depression.

They're awesome, capable, and willing to help. But we have to tell them how.

Next up is a quick guide on what they need to know. I've also put it online, and you're welcome to send them there.

http://inkandfeet.com/support-people

I've also written *How to Help Someone with Depression*, which gives the basics, and higher-level view of what the experience of depression is like.

http://inkandfeet.com/how-to-help-someone-with-depression

Take them, mix it and tweak it and make it *you*. Add the things that will help you when Aunt Dee comes to town.

Let's dive in to the guide!

HOW TO BE AN AWESOME SUPPORT PERSON

PEOPLE

Welcome!

So you want to be an awesome support person, eh?

Hooray! Being an awesome support person for a person who deals with depression is actually pretty easy — though not necessarily intuitive. In this guide, we'll cover everything you need to know.

The Person You're Supporting is Normal

Depression hits one in five people in the world over the course of their lives. It affects one in twenty on a regular basis.

It's in the cards for a lot of humanity, and the person you're supporting happened to get it. This doesn't mean they're crazy or strange.

It means they're the same wonderful person you know, and that every once in a while, a really weird energy-sucking flu comes to town, and they have to deal with some bullshit.

They've reached out to you because they're taking their depression seriously, focusing on living a life they love (in which depression just plays a passing role), and they'd like your help in taking it on.

That's about the sanest, most normal thing I think one person could say to another. :)

But what's that support look like? Let's dig in.

Sit, Ask, Listen

The most effective thing you can do for the person you're supporting is summed up in Sit, Ask, Listen.

Sit — take some time just to sit down with them (physically or virtually), and assure them that you're here for the long haul, you're sticking through the ups and the downs, and that they have real support that's not going away.

Ask — ask how their day is going, but also ask how their depression is going. Dig into the dark corners — are they having any Crazy Thoughts? Really sad things? Be fearless and open in asking how your person is really doing. Focus on open-ended questions without expected outcomes.

Listen — just listen to their response. Don't try to fix it, *do* anything, or give advice. Just listen, empathize, and validate their experiences. "Ugh. That's rough." "That has to feel scary." "Man, depression is such bullshit for you to have to deal with!"

People who struggle with depression typically have no one they can safely talk to about the monster that's eating their life. But the person you're supporting does — you and their other support people.

Just having someone they can talk to about the crazy shit that's happening in their head, and having both of you acknowledge that those are some *crazy fucking thoughts* makes the person you're supporting feel *sane*.

By just sitting and listening, you give them a space where

285

they're no longer tied to their thoughts. The thoughts are a symptom of the crazy energy-sucking flu, and you know about it too, and seriously, WTF kind of flu is this that gives someone Crazy Thoughts? That's some bullshit.

Avoid Giving Advice

One of the most challenging things about being a support person is wanting to give advice, and seeing things that we're sure would help and we're pretty sure the person we're supporting can't see.

But as much as you possibly can, *avoid giving advice.*

It's not that your advice isn't good — it's that the person you're supporting isn't often in a place to receive it, and it comes off as insulting and demeaning.

Managing depression is mostly about managing an energy level. Your person may know that getting out for a walk would help — but they don't have the energy to do it.

For instance, telling them "Hey, you should go for a walk" is likely to just make them feel insulted (they already know that), worthless (they can't even go for a walk), and like reaching out to you was a bad idea (you just make them feel worse).

Your simple, well-meaning, good advice just made things a lot worse.

So as much as you can, resist offering advice unless you're specifically asked for some.

Here's your metaphor:

Treat their life like their car. Only drive when you're asked to.

As a support person, your role is to be a sounding board, a

place for them to get thoughts out of their heads and find perspective, and to reduce isolation. That's it. It's most definitely not to fix them.

Check in Consistently

Put a time on your calendar and just check in. The person you're supporting will give you the specifics of what they need, but in general, every few days is cool for the "good day" parts of depression. On the "really bad" and "false well" days, that's up to probably a couple times a day.

You'll be sharing check-ins with the other folks who are supporting, so it won't all be on you. Coordinate and make it something you can do without it burning you out.

When you check in, you want to make sure to get two answers:

1. What kinds of days are they having?
In this book, we split them up into "good days with depression", "bad days with depression", "really bad days", "false well days", and the lovely "days without depression." Earlier in this book is a good description of each.

Knowing what kind of day they're having will help you know what level of support is needed, and what you need to do to effectively help.

2. How are they doing?
In this space, you're making a space for them to talk qualitatively about how things are going, if they're seeing trends up or down, what they're doing, and just generally get things out.

As noted before, you don't have to fix anything (and it's better if you don't try) — you just have to listen, and make the space for them to be heard.

Pretty simple, right? It really is. And it makes a huge difference!

But let's take one moment and talk about the biggest key to being an effective support person.

Make Reaching Out a Positive Experience

You're checking in and showing you care! That's positive, right?

Yes. But it can quickly turn into a negative space where someone who needs support doesn't reach out because reaching out makes them feel like shit.

This is the hardest thing you have to do.

The challenge isn't what to do — it's what not to do. Be mindful of how you respond, and keep your focus on creating a safe, encouraging space. One where the person you're supporting can show up, talk openly about what's going on, and not feel bad or guilty or wrong for thinking or feeling the way they do.

Your role isn't to fix them — it's to keep them from being isolated. This is why asking probing questions is important. It's easy (and a really natural, learned behavior) for a person with depression to hide the dark stuff and appear "fine."

Pay particular attention to the way you ask questions. Keep them open-ended and make a space where any response is ok. Ask, "How's your depression today?" instead of "Are you feeling better?"

Keeping things open-ended is subtle, but it makes a big difference in easing the burden of response for the person you're supporting.

When you create a space where it's genuinely ok for them to

talk about *anything* without fear, and ask questions about the dark stuff, you're ensuring they aren't isolated — and doing a powerful, powerful thing to help.

Most of all, talking to you should leave them feeling *better*, and they should be glad to have done it. That's what's going to keep them coming back, even in the hard parts, and what makes the biggest difference.

Know What to Expect, and Don't Freak Out

Depression is weird. In the best times, it zaps your energy. In the worst times, it gives you Crazy Thoughts and distorts your view of reality.

It's important for both you and the person you're supporting to understand this:

The Crazy Thoughts are the weird, brain-bending flu of depression, not *them*.

The person you're supporting isn't insane, broken, or damaged. They just have a crazy-ass flu going through their brain, and it's giving them Crazy Thoughts. Think about how you'd react if they had a really high fever, and they were talking gibberish. Depression is like that. It will pass, and the person you're supporting is still themselves.

The real downsides to depression are this:
1. It's a downer, sucks to experience, and puts a bit of weight on the people around the person dealing with it.
2. In rare cases, it can lead to suicide.

Suicide is the one that scares everybody, and the reason that people freak out. Don't freak out.

Suicides are most common in the really bad and "false well" days. Talk it through with the person you're supporting. What do they want you to do to support them? What seems like a good balance?

It's important to know that suicidal thoughts are much more common than attempted suicides. If your person shares that they're having suicidal thoughts, listen, and communicate openly about them, but don't freak out. They often come with the territory on the really bad days.

On those days, the person you're supporting is focused on keeping the perspective that *these are just thoughts*. You need to keep it, too.

Despite what TV ads would lead us to believe, there aren't currently any magic bullet treatments for depression. Good support like yours helps *massively*. Professional help can be useful in certain situations. Medication is a mixed bag, but can be really useful in certain situations.

The person you're supporting has opinions on all those things. Ask them, understand where they're coming from, and allow them a space to voice their opinions and retain agency of their life.

Which brings us to how you'll actually get all those opinions.

Have One Big Conversation

Have one big conversation with the person you're supporting where they tell you what they need, and you get any questions you have answered.

You can do this collectively with the other support people or individually. It's best done when depression isn't around or on a good day.

The goal here is to answer all your questions and to understand what's helpful (and unhelpful) for the person you're supporting.

Here's topics to make sure you cover:

- What things are helpful for them in support
- What to do in the really bad/false well days
- People to avoid contacting or telling about their depression
- If there are any pros on the support team, and how they feel about professional help
- What to do if they express suicidal thoughts
- What their favorite delivery food is
- What things take a lot of energy during depression that they could do
- What their experience of depression is like

Keep the tone open-minded, non-judgmental, and curious. Ask the questions you've got, but keep in mind this may be the first time your person has openly talked through a lot of these questions. Give them the space and time to get their thoughts out and make sense of the space.

As you talk, jot down notes on things you agree on.

When the conversation is done, type them up and send them over to your person, to make sure you understood them correctly and are in agreement on any action points.

This is your binding agreement.

Other Things You Should Know

The stages or types of days of depression.

The person you're supporting will give you a more detailed breakdown in your conversation, but broadly, depression has good days when it's just about low energy, and bad days where a lack of energy is combined with weird cross-wiring of the brain and dark thoughts.

Each visit from depression doesn't necessarily go through all the stages. Often it's just the "good days with depression" and then it's gone.

The worse days don't usually come out of nowhere. They're often combined with the sad or hard things in life like loss, grief, heartbreak, and intense and difficult experiences. If the person you're supporting just reached out and is in a good day, but also just broke up with their ex or experienced a big loss, know and expect they'll probably go through a few of the stages.

What helps your person.

The person you're supporting is the expert on this, and they'll let you know what specific things you can do to be most effective.

Broadly, it's about giving them a space to speak freely, asking probing questions, showing up consistently to check in, and sticking it out with them.

But at some point when they're not experiencing depression, have that conversation on what things generally help them, what doesn't, and what ways you can do the most good.

The person you're supporting is the expert on their depression. Get their advice, and take it.

That mostly, it's about energy level.

Depression is mostly about energy level.

If you can focus on being helpful in one aspect as a support person, focus on helping their energy level — not their mood — their energy level.

One big mistake I see in support people's responses is that they try to make the person feel better right now, today.

They're trying to win the battle. They should be trying to win the war.

Here's an example. During a bad or halfway bad day with depression, my day might be summed up with eating a big salad, working out, and then retiring to the couch to watch *Star Trek* the entire rest of the day. That is actually a great set of actions.

From the outside, this might seem terrible. I haven't left the house, haven't done anything to lift up my mood, and I spent most of my time on the couch.

But actually, my actions were spot on. I spent the little energy I had on two things — eating a salad and working out

— because I knew tomorrow and the next day I'd have more energy because I'd done them.

I spent my energy on getting more energy.

And that's how we win the war.

Optional, but helpful: Experience what it's like.

This is optional, but if you don't experience depression yourself, and want to know what the experience is like, there's nothing better than taking a few minutes, and going through a round of an online game called *Depression Quest*.

http://www.depressionquest.com/

Depression Quest was built specifically to give people who don't experience depression a sense of what it's like in the day to day, and why this book and so many other resources say things like "focus on your energy level" instead of "focus on feeling better."

It can be intense to play through, but as a person who experiences depression regularly, I can tell you that it's also accurate. If you want an insight in, it's worth checking out.

Keep Checking In

A close friend of mine lost his mother unexpectedly. A few years later, we had a mutual friend with a similar loss. I asked him, "What should I do to really effectively support our friend? What helped you?"

"Keep checking in," he said. "Most people do a great job checking in right away. But a month later, they're all gone. Just knowing that someone was keeping an eye on me in the long term made the biggest difference."

The same is true for depression. Keep checking in, even after it's passed.

Put check-ins on your calendar, so you don't forget, and keep checking in a few times after Aunt Dee seems like she's gone, just to be sure. Sometimes she's sneaky.

Trust Each Other

Here's the last thing you need to do. Trust the person you're supporting.

This is also hard to do. But it's important.

Trust them and be explicit in that trust.

If you've made a space where they can talk openly about anything and are checking in regularly, you'll be able to say, "I'm here to help you through all the parts of depression we talked about, and I'm trusting you to tell me what's going on," and have that feel like an honest responsibility, and not a guilt-laden missive.

They also have to trust you. The surest way to lose the trust of a person you're supporting is to reach out to non-support people, and tell them what's going on.

You and your fellow support people have been picked out intentionally. You care and you're capable of understanding your actions, changing, and reacting in a way that's genuinely helpful.

People who are close to your person, but aren't one of their support people were left off that list for a reason — they make the experience of depression *worse* for the person you're supporting.

Trust the person you're supporting, and trust your fellow support people. Together, you are enough.

Touch Base with Other Support People

Make it as easy as possible for the person you're supporting to ask for and get support.

When you're first asked, get the contact information of their other support people, reach out, and say hi.

You don't need to do any sort of planning or complicated strategizing, but *do* say hello, and acknowledge that you're a team in supporting your person.

That little bit of knowing will make things a lot more natural when Aunt Dee rolls into town.

Take Care of Yourself

Being a support person does take energy, effort, and emotional labor.

That reality is a big part of why they have multiple support people with whom you can share the load. If you have things happening in your life and don't have the energy to show up and create that open space, that's ok.

Communicate that with the other support people, coordinate, and get yourself some recharge time. When you're ready to tag back in, come on back.

The same will be true from time to time from the other folks doing support. You're all in this together. Collectively, you can make it.

Advanced: Bring the Energy

I almost didn't include this section, because it's a power move. It's so easy to get wrong, and it can backfire, badly.

But it can also really, really work.

I'd say to avoid trying this unless you're really comfortable with it, you have an established, trusting rapport with the person you're supporting, you know personality-wise, this is the kind of shit you can really pull off, and gut feel, it seems like the right call.

But if all of those are true, give it a shot.

The technique is this: bring in some disruption, energy, and fuel.

This is the other side of the coin to listening and providing a safe space.

It's bringing in high energy, calling things out, and directly confronting their depression and its pull toward the deep.

It's a strong hand up, a slap on the back, and a *"C'mon. We're taking on your depression, beating it, and getting you back to doing* _____. *This is enough of its bullshit."*

Bring that energy and fire, **direct it at their depression**, and make a space for them to get pissed at it, too.

What kind of an asshole disease makes people want to die and have Crazy Thoughts? Fuck that disease. Fuck it having any say over what we do with our lives.

Critically, bringing the energy means bringing enough energy for two people, and getting out and doing something that the person you're supporting loves.

You bringing the energy won't give them any extra — so you'll have to bring enough for both of you and then some.

The list of ways this can go wrong is long, and I do encourage caution.

When you bring the energy and fire, make sure it's *never* directed at the person you're supporting. A quick check is to make sure they can cheer along with everything you're saying and doing.

Great: "Fuck depression!" The person you're supporting will probably think, "Hell yeah, fuck depression!"

Terrible: "Get out of bed and let's go!" Um, no. The person you're supporting will probably think, "Don't you think I would if I could? Ugh. I wish you'd just leave me alone."

In the portrayals we see of depression in movies and TV usually, it's resolved with a big, rousing speech from a close friend.

That speech will not work, and the movies are lying.

Depression is almost never written accurately because a slow, hard-to-notice recovery makes for poor climactic sequences. If you're thinking, "Like that speech on _____", stop. Not like that speech.

Instead, what you're doing is assisted behavioral activation. You're helping your person experience the things they love without spending any of their very little energy.

Do not think of this as a quick fix. There are no quick fixes.

To reiterate, this is a power move, and there's a lot of places it can go disastrously wrong, destroy the trust you've built as a support person (and your friendship), and *hurt* the person you're trying to support. If you have even slight misgivings, don't try it. Seriously. Don't try it.

But if you have the personality, energy, and perspective to do it, done right, there's almost nothing as effective in picking someone up.

PEOPLE

It's Not Usually that Big of a Burden

After all of the above, it may seem like you're being asked to carry half the moon for a person you care about.

You're not. The intensity of this section was intentional, to be clear that when your person needs your support, they *really need* your support, and they need it in the specific way we've just talked through.

But if they're reaching out to you, odds are pretty good that their depression is being managed pretty well. Depression is a disease that can tend to snowball — so the earlier it's caught and dealt with, the better.

The fact that the person you're supporting reached out to set up a support structure at all means they're taking their depression seriously, and the odds of them spending a huge amount of time in the really bad places are pretty low.

But just in case it does happen, they'll know you and their other support people will be there to help them find their feet, and get back up.

You're all set — that's all you need to know to be an awesome support person! On behalf your person, and me — thanks!

USING YOUR SUPPORT PEOPLE

How to Use Your Support People

Alright, so you've got some support people, and you've prepared them for what to expect.

But how do you use them in practice? You just put a flag up.

If, one day, you notice Aunt Dee has come to town, you just reach out to one of your support people and tell them what kind of day you're in.

That's it.

They'll take it from there and follow up in the ways you've both talked through until Aunt Dee's sorry butt has left the premises.

Reach Out For Help Earlier Than You Need It

Because depression is weird, and can tend to bend the brain, you'll want to be proactive about reaching out.

Tell your support people earlier than you think you should, and give them a heads up if you're heading into something that you think is going to trigger you.

For example, when I started writing this book, I reached out to my support people.

"I'm finally writing that book on depression," I told them. "I'm pretty sure it's going to trigger every single thing I have around it, wreck me, and make me a melange of depressed, angry that anyone has to deal with this shit, and oddly optimistic. I need you to check in with me, and help me remain mindful."

They did, and though the process still threw me to the mat a few times, knowing that there were people checking in, listening, and offering a hand back up made a huge difference.

There will be things in your life that you know might trigger your depression — places and people that are tied with memories of past episodes. Grief. Certain seasons or experiences.

As you stalk your depression, you'll get to know that list better and better. Some you'll be able to avoid. Others you'll just see coming — and you'll know to reach out to your support people in advance.

Alright. Now you've got some great support people (and if you don't yet, consider reaching out to at least one person before you move on to the next chapter).

But what about folks who aren't your support people, that you still interact with? Let's talk about them.

HANDLING EVERYONE ELSE

Anti-Support People

Anti-support people are the well-meaning people who say all the wrong things, and think that they're helping.

They are *terrible*.

They're people who say things like "Suck it up" or "It's not that bad" or "I have blue days too."

Their sentences begin with "At least…" or "Maybe tomorrow…" or "I'm sure there will be better days."

The worst of these sorts of folks are the well-meaning types who we're close to. People who really care (our #1 for support), but who aren't able to understand that their reactions and behaviors are making things worse (no #2).

Often, these folks look like close family members or friends, or random sort-of-friends on facebook.

They're one of the worst influences to have around when depression is in town, because you have to spend some of the very little energy you have dealing with and supporting *them*, instead of putting it toward caring for yourself or doing things you value and love.

Even worse, their "help" often comes with guilt, anxiety, and panicked uncertainty.

The best thing you can do with them?

Ditch 'em.

Seriously.

While depression's in town, just ditch everyone who isn't one of your support people.

Doesn't matter if they're your mom, your close friend, or the president of your social club. If they bug you for a response, tell 'em you're slammed and that you'll get back to them in a week or two. Then let them go.

This isn't a crazy Machiavellian idea — it's just a reality.

As we talked about back at the beginning, you've got a small fraction of your normal energy. (Remember those spoons?) Those people are going to take it without giving you support back.

For the moment, take a break from them.

They'll still be there when Aunt Dee has left town.

Seriously. When depression comes to town, tell these folks, "Hey, I'm really busy, but I'll get back to you in a few weeks when the smoke clears."

If you'd feel more comfortable telling them Aunt Dee's in town, you can say, "I've got a visit from depression, and I've contacted my support people, and I have good support. I don't have any spare energy right now, but I'm ok, and we'll talk more in a little while when I'm on the upswing. Thanks for understanding and giving me space."

Regardless of how you do it, intentionally let them go for a little while.

Save your spoons for things that get you more spoons.

Family and Friends

You'll also have other folks who are family or friends who don't fall into either category.

They're not one of your support people, but they're also not one of the super-annoying "look on the bright side" anti-support folks.

For close folks who fall into this middle category, for the most part, just put them on mute for a little while.

This is a thing we naturally do when depression comes to town anyway — we don't respond to texts, emails, and the like, and we hibernate a little.

As long as you've reached out to your support people, this is a totally normal and perfectly OK reaction.

You're saving your spoons for things that let you get more spoons.

If you feel like putting off replies to the texts and emails until Aunt Dee has left town, put them off. All of these folks will still be there when she's gone, and they won't think twice about the delay.

We'll cover this in more detail in the next chapter, but if someone really needs a response, tell 'em that you're dealing with the flu, and you'll get back to them soon.

It's all good, and all of them will totally understand.

Coworkers and Classmates, Teachers and Bosses

What about everyday life, with people you don't necessarily want to have a long, intense conversation about depression with?

Tell 'em you're getting over a rough flu.

Honestly. The external symptoms are the same (low energy, looking a bit rough), the care is the same (do less, take care of yourself), and if your depression happens to come with bouts of crying, it'll even explain the puffy eyes.

And everyone gets the flu. People will understand, and give you a break.

Tell 'em you're getting over the flu. It's really that simple.

Other Folks You Know

As for everyone else — the comment warriors on Facebook, the nosy neighbor, and the super chatty person at your church or social club?

Ditch 'em.

While your depression is around — provided you've reached out to your support people — if you can ditch people, ditch them.

Remember the spoons. If you think the interaction is going to energize you and give you more spoons, go for it! But if you think you'll just be drained, give it a pass.

You have a get-out-of-tiring-shit-free card, right here. Use it.

Random Strangers

Finally, there are the strangers on the bus, in the line at the grocery store, and otherwise out and about in public.

There are two approaches that can be great for these folks, and you can use them interchangeably, depending on how you feel.

Option 1: Engage

Strangers can actually be a great way to engage with the world and give yourself a little bit of energy and lift without the risk, because they have no strings attached.

A short little conversation with the checkout person at your grocery store can be a great reminder that people are pretty lovely, and that you don't actually look like you're falling apart — but without any of the responsibility to carry that conversation forward, explain yourself, or worry about the consequences.

Interactions with strangers can let you break out of Aunt Dee's narratives for moment, and have a clear, unfiltered interaction.

Sometimes they're great. When you're not feeling it,

Option 2: Avoid

This has actually become really, really easy in the past few years.

Just stare at your phone.

It's simple, it will always work, and nobody will bug you. Scroll through emails or texts, play bubble-popper, or fake browse *The New York Times*. (Avoid Facebook and the like if you can — it's been shown to amplify depression.)

But if you need a little space out in public, just grab your phone, look down, and *voilà*, you've got it.

That covers strangers. There's one last group that you might choose to interact with — the pros.

THE
PROS

PEOPLE

Professional Help

The only thing that seems to have more stigma than depression itself are the health professionals who treat it.

And honestly, that really, really sucks, because those folks are super helpful in taking on depression.

You should always go with what you're comfortable with.

But do also know that in addition to close people you know, you can also tack on medical professionals in to your support group.

They're great, and they've got a few tools that even the best support people don't know how to use.

There are a huge number of mental health professionals from a variety of disciplines, and a gazillion long-winded books on finding good mental health professionals. I'm not going to bore you with another one.

Instead, here's my short and simple perspective on finding an effective professional support person.

Go for Competency

One of the big tropes is that you have to spend three months seeing a dozen therapists until you get one with whom you have a great "connection". I think this is utter bullshit.

Find a therapist who feels really, really competent. Someone who knows what they're doing, and inspires confidence. Go with them.

You wouldn't pick your surgeon based on if they seemed friendly. You'd pick on whether they seemed like they were a *damn good surgeon*. The same principles apply here.

Now, before my inbox fills up with angry mail from therapists, let me be explicit on what the body of research says.

There *is* a positive effect from having a therapist you really connect with. The literature calls it the "therapeutic alliance", and in general, the stronger the feeling of connection, the more benefit folks get out of the interaction.

But — the research also shows that a great connection doesn't make up for poor technique. Think back to those graphs of helpfulness we looked at way back in the beginning. Closeness and helpfulness are not necessarily linked things.

What you really want is someone who's highly competent who you *also* connect with. And in great news, it's actually easier to find those folks today than it's ever been.

To make things simple, when you're looking, start with practitioners who use a current, evidence-based framework (we'll talk about them next). The fact that someone's staying current on the latest things we know about taking on depression indicates that they're pretty likely to be competent.

Then, if you'd like, have a quick phone chat with a few of them, and trust your gut. Go with whichever person feels best to you.

Go For Validated Techniques

We're fortunate to have several models of therapy that are backed by lots of scientific research, have been shown to work, and have consistent training and frameworks.

The most proven three are Acceptance and Commitment Therapy (ACT), Cognitive Behavioral Therapy (CBT), and Dialectical Behavioral Therapy (DBT). All three are shown to work in treating depression.

My personal preference is ACT, since I think it's a better fit for most experiences of depression (where acceptance and action can play a dynamic role in improving life). For some folks' depression though, CBT or DBT is a better choice.

All of them are radically different than the "sit on the couch and tell me your feelings" sort of therapy most people think of. I've used ACT myself, and it's really, really good, and it works. Here's a link to a search for providers:

inkandfeet.com/act-providers

There's also the cost. Happily, a lot of providers will do flexible payment plans, and most insurance companies cover visits.

But if money's tight and you don't have insurance, there are also workbooks that are solid substitutes, and they're cheap.

For ACT, I highly recommend either *Get Out of Your Mind and Into Your Life* by Steven C. Hayes or *The Happiness Trap* by Russ Harris.

If you're trying out professional help, feel free to try each framework or talk them through with your pro, and see what works for you. But pick one of those three frameworks — they've been tried, tested, and actually work.

When to reach out for professional help? Actually, it turns out there are two great times.

Calling the Pros When You're in a Scary Place

When you're in the "really bad" or the "false well" days, your support people are going to be awesome, but they may also be out of their depth.

You'll have experiences that they probably haven't seen before, and more than anything, they're just going to want to do the right thing and help you out.

It may make sense for you to add a professional to your support people to help guide you through those hard spots, or authorize your support people to make that call on your behalf.

The biggest advantage a mental health professional has is *experience.* They've not only seen what you're going through before, they spent years of their life training, learning, and working to understand how to effectively help people in just these situations.

It's the same as going to a heart surgeon when you've got a heart condition. There's a time and place for specialists, and one of those times can be when you're in the "really bad" or "false well" days.

Don't be afraid to get backup. I can tell you from personal experience that almost all of those people are lovely human beings, and effective at helping you out.

And there's one other situation where it might make sense to reach out to a professional.

Calling the Pros When You're in an Awesome Place

Yep. Reaching out when you're not experiencing depression at all.

Crazy, right? Here's why.

If you choose to reach out when you're doing well and not experiencing depression, you can just sit down and pick their brain about the sort of tools you can use in combatting your depression.

You can get personalized, expert advice on how to build your support systems, the sorts of things that will motivate and help you, and the particular things that you, specifically, should keep an eye on.

Seeing a mental health professional when I was doing well was the single best move I ever made in taking on my depression.

It took me *25 years* of dealing with depression before I was ready to do it, but once I did, I was so, so glad I'd given it a shot.

It was the single most effective thing I've ever done in taking on my depression.

Most folks tend to think that mental health folks are only for when you're in a rough spot. I'm here to tell you the opposite.

They're at their very best — and most impactful on your life — when you're well.

That's Everybody

That rounds out the people section, and that covers pretty much everyone in our lives.

You now have the tools to identify, recruit, and collaborate with some great support people to help you through visits from Aunt Dee.

You have techniques to handle family and friends, your boss and coworkers, and that annoying friend on facebook. You're even ready for that chatty grocery store cashier.

You've also got a good handle on when the pros can be useful, and when it might make sense to bring one onto your support team.

You're in fantastic shape. You've got all the tools you'll need to handle your depression when it comes and get back to a life you love.

Now, it's time we looked at the long game.

THE LONG GAME

The Long Game

We've been through a lot so far. Talking about what depression is. Starting to build your toolbox. Understanding tools you can use to take actions, use your mind, change your environment, get great support people, and talk about depression. We've talked through the deep dark places, and what to do about them.

Now we're going to talk about one last piece — the best one of all — the long game.

We're going to talk about your life stretching forward over the years ahead, an awesome life filled with adventure, meaning, love, joy, sorrow, and value. A life well-lived.

It will be a life that, as a small side bar, has depression too.

But in the scope of your broader life, that attribute will turn out to be a bigger positive than negative.

Let's dig in.

LIVING FOR THE LONG TERM

A Funny Thing about People with Depression

You'd think that depression is all bad, that it's terrible luck, and it makes our lives worse.

But it's not true.

Like most things, depression is double-edged.

Yes, it sucks to deal with, and all of the scary and difficult things we've talked about in this book are true.

But something else is, too.

People who deal with depression tend to live more fulfilled lives.

Maybe it's because we've faced down the scary monsters in the deep dark places, come out alive, and after that, nothing really seems truly scary.

Maybe it's because we've experienced a world that's been drained of all its color, and when the color came back, we knew how to appreciate it.

Maybe it's because we had to think about all the people around us, our relationships, and evaluate them on their merits — and it's meant we surrounded ourselves with people who are better for us, and whom we're better for.

Maybe it's because we've had to count our spoons, and learned to be conscious of how we spend our energy.

Probably, it's a combination of all of the above.

But taken together, a person who is fearless, present in the joy and sorrows of life, has wonderful people around them, and knows how to spend their energy on what matters — yeah, that person can do pretty much anything they set their mind to.

And that's you.

Depression has saddled some tremendous difficulties on your back. But as you learn to navigate and build a life you love that includes depression, you'll also pick up some powerful skills that most people will never learn.

Those skills kind of make you a bad-ass.

And as a result, even including the visits from Aunt Dee, your life will be more full and more fully-lived.

Depression is a part of your challenges in life. But it's also a part of what makes you great.

Live a Values-Driven Life

As we talked about back in the Behavioral Activation tool, one of the best ways to combat depression is by taking actions that line up with your values, even when you're feeling bad.

But happily, taking actions that line up with your values also happens to be a fantastic way to live your life.

Living this way means that you focus your time and energy on the things that really matter to you, instead of the things that come up and fade, or flicker in the wind.

It also tends to mean that Aunt Dee stops by less often.

A life filled with the things you care about and less of Aunt Dee? That's as big a win-win as I've ever heard.

There are a lot of tools for identifying your values and putting them in action.

One of my favorites to find them is an exercise that's been tested and scientifically validated for three decades.

I'm including the full exercise in the next chapter, and you can also download it here:

http://inkandfeet.com/values-exercise

Give it a shot, find the values that really matter to you, and then get started bringing them to life in your day-to-day living.

Find Your Values Exercise

Values are the ideas and principles that we hold most dearly. They're different for every person, and they can even shift and change over the course of our lives.

But in terms of planning out what you want to do with your life, they're one of the best compasses we have.

In the exercise below, we'll explore and identify your most closely-held values — the ones you should build your life around.

But before we do, I want to take a quick detour, and talk about the Happiness Myth.

The Happiness Myth
For most of us, if we're asked what we'd like the next few years of our lives to be like, "I want to be happy" would probably make the list. It's totally normal and natural.

But it doesn't work.

In practice, we can't really go after happiness, because it's not a place or an actionable thing. It's a state of being, caused by where we are, who we're around, and what we're doing.

Since it's not a place we can get to, chasing after happiness by itself is likely to leave us exhausted and empty-handed.

So what to do instead? Focus on our values.

Let's say one of your core values is justice — to promote fair and equal treatment for all.

Knowing that, you can go out in the world, and work on things that promote equality. And when you're out in the world, taking actions that lead to equality and fair treatment, you guessed it — you're going to feel happy.

Going after happiness on its own may not work, but going after the things that are aligned with what you care about — that does.

Ok. So now we know why understanding your values can be a really useful thing. But what exactly are your values?

Turns out, there's a great, well-tested exercise to find that out.

Here's how to do it.

Find Your Values

This is a four-part process, and to get the most out of it, it's important that you don't read ahead to future steps.

Read the instructions for the step you're on, complete it, then come on back. No peeking. :)

Part One: Sort the List of Values

1. Download this PDF of values cards.
    inkandfeet.com/values-cards

2. Print out the PDF, and cut apart the cards. You'll end up with a good pile of them. (If you don't have a printer, there are modifications just below.)

3. On your floor or a big table, put three notes near the top, saying, "Very important to me," "Important to me," and "Not important to me." It should look something like this:

4. For each card, place it into one of the three columns. When you're trying to figure out which column a card should go in, compare it to the other values you've already put down.

5. When you have all the cards down, read through each of the columns, and feel out if there's anything out of place. Move things around until it feels like an accurate representation of your values.

6. Go on to Part Two!

Modifications if you don't have access to a printer:

No printer? No problem. You can make do without one, and get the same benefits. Here's how:

1. At the top of three pages (or in three columns) write, "Very important to me," "Important to me," and "Not important to me."

2. Reference the PDF, and as you go through, write each value in one of the three columns. You'll end up with something like this:

VERY IMPORTANT TO ME	IMPORTANT TO ME	NOT IMPORTANT TO ME
——————	————	∼∼∼∼∼
——————	∼∼∼∼∼	————
——————	∼∼∼∼∼	————
	∼∼∼∼∼	————
	————	
	————	

3. As you go through the exercise, keep the PDF handy, so you can reference the longer descriptions.

4. Follow the same steps as above.

362

Part Two: Get Specific

Alright, here's where it starts to get good — and get hard. Here are the steps for part two:

1. Take the "Not important to me" and "Important to me" cards, stack them up, and put them to the side.

2. Take the "Very important to me" cards, and stack them up.

3. Do the same exercise we did in part one, but just using your "Very important" cards.

   Separate them into "Not important to me," "Important to me," and "Very important to me" piles. Yep, this is going to hurt. But keep going, and like before, compare the importance of each values to the other things in that column.

4. When you have all the cards down, read through each of the columns, and feel out if there's anything out of place. Move things around until it feels like an accurate representation of your values.

5. Great job. Go on to Part Three!

Part Three: Your Core Values

If by some miracle you have 5 or fewer cards in your "Very important to me" column, you can skip this step! These are your core values. Go on to Part Four.

But if you're like the rest of us, and part two really hurt and you've still got a ton of Very importants, it's time for part three. Let's dig in.

1. Take the "Not important to me" and "Important to me" cards, stack them up, and put them to the side.

2. Take the "Very important to me" cards, and stack them up.

3. Make two columns: "Very important to me" and "Also something I want in my life."

4. Take all the cards you have left and put them in one of the two columns. However, there is one rule.

5. You may only have up to 5 cards in the "Very important to me" column.

6. When you're down to five cards in your "Very important to me" column, you're done.

Completely off-color tip: When I get stuck in this part, I'll sometimes subtitle the columns "Fuck yeah" and "I like this too" The idea is to break me out of the importance mindset, and get in touch with my base, gut-level feelings. What are the things that at my core of cores, I feel strongly enough to swear about?

When you've got your five, you made it! The hard part is over. Go on to Part Four to wrap it up.

Part Four: Make a Record

If you're like me, you'll want to do this values exercise from time to time — I do it myself once a year — and it's nice to have a record.

So, somewhere you'll be able to find it later, write yourself a note and include the longer definitions from the cards:

On ___today's date___, my core values were:
 • Purpose - to have meaning and direction in my life.
 •
 •
 •
 •

Great work. I know this process can be a mix of exciting, enlightening, and excruciating, but it's also immensely valuable in figuring out what we really care about, and where we should focus our energy.

As you look for actions to take on depression and build your life around, come back and reference these values — they're the core of what you care about most.

Make a Two-Year Life Plan

Building on your values, another great tool in taking on your depression and pulling you out of the deep spots is having solid long-term goals you believe in and are working toward.

I'm a big fan of a two-year life plan. It's a short enough time that it inspires movement and action (even when depression is in town), but it's long enough that almost anything is really possible.

As you create systems to support you, consider making a handful of specific long-term goals that you'll work for every day, and putting them up on your wall.

They're a powerful rebuttal when Aunt Dee comes to town. "There," you can point, "that is what I'm doing with my life. Get out of here!"

I run an online course on creating a two-year life plan, and this deep sense of purpose is one of the things I hear most from participants.

Whether you try my system, someone else's, or make your own, consider constructing a specific set of goals for yourself, two years from today.

Note: If you are interested in my course, please use "nobullshitbook" to get a special discount on it just for people like you who bought the book. :) You can check out the details at inkandfeet.com/masterclass. I'd love to see you there.

Never Let Up

It probably goes without saying, but I'm going to say it anyway.

Never let up on your depression.

Because of the way the brain works, the pathways in your mind that caused the symptoms of your depression are never gone. They can become remote, cobweb-filled corridors that you never go down anymore, but they're always there.

Some big things that happen in all our lives — loss, grief, sorrow, heartbreak, and even some smaller things like hunger, music, or a certain smell can all cause our brains to head down those hallways again.

Throughout our lives, even as depression becomes a smaller and smaller part of our everyday existence, we have to remember it exists, and keep our support systems up to date.

But when we do that, we almost assure that when those events come, we'll come out of them just fine.

SHARE YOUR STORY

Share What You Know

As you grow in your life, and feel more and more confidence in the tools you have in dealing with depression, consider sharing your knowledge with the broader world.

Because the reality is this:

You know what you are, as a person who lives with visits from depression and a values-driven, powerful life?

An expert.
A role model.
A person people around you need to hear from.

One in five people deals with a major visit from depression in their lives, and one in twenty deal with it regularly.

Share what you know. Become an awesome support person for someone you know. Build awareness around depression, and share the things that work for you.

We're all in this together, and we can all use your insights and your support.

Be a Support Person

Depression is common enough that you probably know someone else who deals with it.

If so, consider offering to be a support person for them. With the first-hand knowledge you have, and the understanding you've gained in this book on how to be an effective support person, you'd be great at the job.

It's also wonderfully empowering to know that your experiences in dealing with Aunt Dee can be useful and strengthening to someone you know who deals with her, too.

Look around your life, and if you see someone who struggles with it some time, offer them a hand, and explain what a good support person does. (Maybe even lend them your copy of this book, so they get it!)

A quick side note: the hardest part of being a great support person for you *by far* will be holding back all the good stuff you've learned on what helps with your depression.

Remember: Sit, Ask, Listen. When the person you're supporting *asks you* for your advice, that's when it's time to give it.

Talk to Other People About Your Journey

One of the toughest things about depression is its isolation and its stigmatization.

But we can break it.

I am a writer, and a man living with depression. It does not define me, it's simply a part of my life.

The same is true for you. You are out there living your amazing, admirable life, one that happens to include depression. It does not define you.

This book is part of my way to tell people about my journey. To say "Hey, I deal with that too, and I'm over here doing interesting things."

Find the ways that are right for you to tell people about your journey, a way that lets them see that your amazing full life isn't defined by depression, it's just a part of your experience of the world.

Maybe it's a facebook or blog post. Maybe a speech. Maybe a toast over a holiday dinner.

Find the way that's right for you, and let your story out. I'll bet anything that someone who hears it will be really glad you did.

Be an Ambassador

Finally, if you're game, step forward and tell your story on a bigger stage.

Allow the fact that you deal with depression to be a part of your public persona.

Be a visible, active, capable, wonderful human being who is doing things in the world, who says, "I deal with depression too."

We are too silent, too secret about a disease that hits one in five people. It's time that stopped and we all acknowledged depression for what it is — a really common, normal part of life for a huge, huge number of people.

That will take people with courage like you and me standing up and saying, "I have depression." But it can happen, and as a world, we need you.

So let's stand up together, take the stigma out, and show everyone what people with depression are really like:

Amazing.

THANK
YOU

Thank you.

Thank you for reading, listening, and trusting me to share what I know.

I hope this book has helped you in getting a set of tools to take on your depression, and go after your authentic, amazing life.

I wish you a life filled with all the stuff you really love, and that Aunt Dee never stays so long she stains the couch.

Be well,

-Steven

RESOURCES
AND
RESEARCH

Awesome Resources

There are some tremendous people doing and making amazing things in and around depression, some of whom I've mentioned throughout this book.

I'd be completely remiss if I didn't give you their perspectives, talents, and brilliant senses of humor — so here's an all-in-one-place list of some awesome.

The Oatmeal, on what I'd call a Values-Driven Life
http://theoatmeal.com/comics/unhappy

Hyperbole and a Half's brilliantly funny and spot-on comic on the experience of depression.
https://inkandfeet.com/hyperbole

Jenny Lawson aka The Bloggess, on the truth of invisible diseases like depression:
https://inkandfeet.com/bloggess

The Awkward Yeti's wonderful comics on depression:
https://inkandfeet.com/yeti

Christine Miserando, creator of Spoon Theory:
https://inkandfeet.com/spoon-theory

Depression Quest, by Zöe Quinn:
http://www.depressionquest.com/

Katy Davis's awesome animations of Brené Brown's talk that explain listening and empathy:
http://inkandfeet.com/brene

And finally, the article that started this whole thing:
https://inkandfeet.com/how-to-help-someone-with-depression

Note: The links above will redirect you to their sites, even though it looks like most of them are on my site. This way just lets me have links in the book that are easy to type, and that I know will stay good even if those articles move in the future.

Finding the Latest Research

The landscape of research on depression is huge and changing pretty rapidly. Every day, we learn new things on how depression works inside our brains and bodies, and hone the tools and techniques we have to take it on.

Because of that pace of progress, I've decided to forgo a quickly-outdated reference page, and replace it with some general advice that will hold up a lot better.

If you're looking to learn more or stay current on the latest research on depression, your best bet is to turn to the pros.

Start by finding a competent, passionate therapist in your city who practices the framework you're interested in.

Sit down over some coffee, and ask where they're reading new information and what publications they follow to stay current. Pick their brains on new papers that have come out and the current landscape of research.

Then, start your learning *there*.

Behavioral research is vast and dense, and if you'd like to dive in, having some companions to show you the ropes can help immensely.

Also — and I speak from experience — geeking out with those folks is a whole lot of fun.

Enjoy the journey!

-Steven

CPSIA information can be obtained
at www.ICGtesting.com
Printed in the USA
BVOW03s1141171017
497902BV00001B/8/P